Kitesurfing in the waves

The Complete Guide

2/23/12
$39.95

Kitesurfing in the waves

The Complete Guide

Kristin Boese and Christian Spreckels

Translated by Julie Roberts

WILEY ✦ NAUTICAL

Wavekiting mit Kristin Boese
Christian Spreckels

Copyright © 2008 by Verlag pietsch, Postfach 103742, 70032 Stuttgart.
A company of Paul Pietsch-Verlage GmbH & Co. Originally published in German.
ISBN 978-3-613-50581-0. All rights reserved.

Authorised English Translation © 2009 John Wiley & Sons Ltd

Registered office
John Wiley & Sons Ltd, The Atrium, Southern Gate, Chichester, West Sussex, PO19 8SQ, United Kingdom

For details of our global editorial offices, for customer services and for information about how to apply for permission to reuse the copyright
material in this book please see our website at www.wiley.com.

Library of Congress Cataloging-in-Publication Data

Boese, Kristin, 1977-
Kitesurfing in the waves : the complete guide / Kristin Boese and Christian Spreckels.
p. cm.
Includes bibliographical references.
ISBN 978-0-470-74678-3 (pbk. : alk. paper)
1. Kite surfing. I. Spreckels, Christian. II. Title.
 GV840.K49B64 2009
 797.3—dc22
 2009009710

A catalogue record for this book is available from the British Library.
Paperback ISBN: 978-0-470-74678-3

Typeset by Stephen Dent, Bath, UK.
Printed and bound by SNP Leefung Printers Ltd, China.

Contents

6

Introduction

Kitesurfing in the waves is the perfect symbiosis of two water sports — surfing and kitesurfing. At the same time, this new sport takes surfing, a pastime dating back over 1000 years, into a new dimension. It goes without saying that surfing is the "mother of all water sports", yet its development in recent decades to take kitesurfing into the waves is entirely logical. This is because the possibilities opened up by tow-in surfing appeared to mark the end of surfing's evolution; but then the use of the kite was introduced, combining kitesurfing with wave riding and revolutionizing the sport once again. More and more surfers are now using a kite in pursuit of their sport. This could be because using the kite heightens the sporting challenge of wave riding and makes it possible to get even more out of it. Additionally, a growing number of kitesurfers are seeking a new dimension to their sport by kiting in waves.

We'll come back to this combination of the oldest and youngest water sports and the developments leading to it later in Part 1 of this book. Along with useful information, such as knowing what you need in order to practise this sport and how wind arises and generates waves, we'll consider another very important point — the choice of where to go kitesurfing in the waves. The first section also describes the safety measures required and offers advice on long- and short-term training strategies, which in conjunction with mental imaging will make it easier to learn the surfing basics and tricks.

In the second part of the book, various basics and tricks are introduced with the aid of detailed photo sequences; these are broken down into their essential elements and the important key points for the mental imaging process. All manoeuvres are listed in ascending order according to their degree of difficulty, a practice that has proved valuable in training. You can therefore look for new basics and tricks suited to your level of ability and the conditions, and practise them intensively following the same pattern.

In Part III, we offer tips on activities and workout routines that you can follow when it isn't possible to go kitesurfing. These relate to the learning or training effects that can be achieved by practising similar sports, and also to body conditioning exercises. We'll also look at the equipment used.

It doesn't matter whether you're a surfer or a kiter, all the information and advice offered in this book will help you to not only learn quickly and safely how to kitesurf in the waves, but also to recreate the deeply satisfying experience enjoyed by the wave-riding kings of Oceania over 1000 years ago — the unique experience of riding a wave skilfully, in our case using a kite.

We wish you lots of fun and success in your quest!

Kristin Boese and Christian Spreckels

Part 1: Before kitesurfing in the waves

Kitesurfing in the waves should be regarded as a further development of the sport of surfing – not just from a historical perspective, but also from the point of view of kinesiology, the science of human movement. First we'll pick up on this interesting aspect of its historical development and then we'll take a look at other aspects worth mentioning.

1 Interesting facts, useful info

A young sport with a long history

As a sport of the new millennium, it's clear that kitesurfing in the waves is the present; that it will also be the sport of the future is a view shared by more than just kiting enthusiasts. What is remarkable here is the merging of the most recent water sport with the oldest: wave riding. This was considered the sport of kings over 1000 years ago, for although members of all social classes used to ride the billowing waves in Oceania at that time, only the kings had the right to surf on certain beaches and to use special surfboards. However, the origins of surfing lie not just in Polynesia, as is often claimed, but are also to be found throughout Oceania and on the west coast of Africa, namely in Senegal and Ghana. Here the art of surfing spread independently of its development in Oceania. But where the sport was first practised remains a mystery. Europeans only learned to surf hundreds of years later, after Captain Cook discovered the sport on his travels in Hawaii in 1777 and brought news of it back to Europe.

With the arrival of missionaries and the spread of European influence throughout Oceania in the 19th century, the sport disappeared for a time due to the introduction of regular working hours and a dwindling interest in the traditional ways of life. It was only at the beginning of the 20th century that surfing was rediscovered as a pastime by school pupils in Honolulu. In 1907 it arrived on the American mainland, and was then introduced into Australia by Duke Kahanamoku in 1915. After this the sport began to spread worldwide, although it wasn't until the 1950s that it turned into a boom – and a surfing fraternity of 5000 exploded into two or three million within five years. Surfing evolved from a sport into a lifestyle characterized by the rejection of the prevailing social norms, and it quickly spilled over into Europe.

Hundreds of years ago, wave riding was taken very seriously, particularly in Hawaii and Tahiti, and this attitude was reflected in the formal framework of the competitions. In these competitions, the fastest surf rides out to a target marker were judged or prizes were awarded for the longest rides. It is known that on Easter Island the best surfer was considered to be the one who rode the biggest and most dangerous waves: "Surfers in big waves must go out to prove to themselves that they are not afraid" (v. Dyke, in Lenk 1972, p. 113). Although this view has persisted, an additional consideration is that only big, fast and therefore potentially dangerous waves make very athletic manoeuvres possible.

To enhance the performance aspect of surfing, a lot of work went into developing surfboards. Over 20 years before the invention of thruster fins[1] revolutionized surfing, so-called "guns" were developed in 1958 at the home of big wave surfing in Waimea Bay. Due to their long, narrow shape, these boards stood out on account of the smooth ride they offered even at high speeds. In big, particularly steep waves such as in Waimea Bay and also at the world-famous big wave spot Maverick's in northern California, the guns constituted a major advance. In parallel with this development, it was observed that surfers were using increasingly shorter and more flexible boards for less steep waves. But in general there was just one aim: to surf ever bigger and more powerful waves.

A big wave community centred around Greg Noll focused exclusively on awaiting the swell of the century and surfing it. On 4 December 1969, the biggest swell ever recorded on Hawaii's North Shore rolled in. This was the day on which surfers paddled into and rode the biggest waves ever, making surfing history. However, this was also the day on which the limits of "paddle surfing" became clear. Paddling into bigger, steeper waves was unthinkable.

It wasn't long, however, before a new

9

development and a new challenge came along. The big wave surfers Darrick Doerner, Buzzy Kerbox and Laird Hamilton fitted footstraps to their boards, as on windsurfing boards, and attached a line to their jet ski, which then towed them into the waves. This form of surfing, termed "tow-in surfing", enabled them to tackle even bigger, steeper waves. Eliminating the need to paddle meant that boards became shorter again, and their manoeuvrability meant that over time increasingly radical manoeuvres became possible.

The challenge of surfing 15-metre-high waves offered the opportunity, as big wave surfer Mickey Muñoz put it, "to discover oneself". Many years later, big wave legend Laird Hamilton's ride at Teahupo'o on the most powerful wave ever, seemingly defying all the laws of physics, earned him the ultimate recognition among the pioneers of big

wave riding: "That's impossible, how can he do that?"[2] This ride went down in surfing history as the most famous ride of all time.

The pressing question at this point was: Had the thousand-year development of this sport thus come to an end? The answer to that question is the sport of the new millennium: kitesurfing in the waves; because as a symbiosis of the sports of surfing and kitesurfing, it opens up entirely new possibilities for the surfer. Not only can a wave kiter get through the shorebreak and out into the line-up far more easily than a surfer or windsurfer, he also catches considerably more waves during a session, and above all catches them more easily. Added to this, the kite's propulsion enables him to bridge slower sections, and his rides become longer as a result. Going back to the sport of kings,

---

[1] The offset arrangement of three fins invented by Australian Simon Anderson in 1980 gave boards improved lateral stability.

[2] Greg Noll.

this was the decisive criterion for judging wave rides all those years ago.

Today, however, this is not the only criterion. Manoeuvres are skilfully executed on the steepest part of the wave, the kite acting as the perfect aid to powerful, dynamic, radical wave riding and enabling the rider to throw large fans of spray.

In their drive to do what they do, surfers and wave kiters are probably riding the same wave, so to speak: in both sports it's the mystical pull associated with the transience and uniqueness of each wave that evokes the virtually indescribable feeling of euphoria that comes from riding a wave successfully. This one wave on which the surfer rides, with or without a kite, may have travelled for days and thousands of miles across the ocean to break finally on this one beach or at this one point, after which it is a thing of the past. No wave is like any other wave ever was or ever will be. Perhaps, though, it is solely the sporting challenge that demands everything of the surfer and drives him on in the search for the perfect wave. The wave changes continually, requiring the surfer to be constantly alert and to make split-second decisions. These must always be made depending on the wave and in relation to the wind when surfing with a kite. If this is achieved successfully even in challenging situations, the surfer forgets everything around him and around the wave – he is "in the zone". Referring to this phenomenon, Jeff Clark, the big wave surfer who discovered Maverick's, said that he concentrated to such an extent while surfing and was so "in tune with the ocean, which he felt with every fibre of his being", that he became "a part of it". And this feeling is the same today as it will be tomorrow and as it was hundreds of years ago; even if this state of complete and utter absorption in an action hasn't always been known as "flow"[3], the blissful

contentment that it brings will have felt the same.

What do you need?

The most important prerequisite for kitesurfing in the waves is kiting. This may sound trivial, but it needs to be clearly emphasized here, because there are always novices out there who want to learn the sport directly without having any experience of kitesurfing. However, it has proved essential to learn how to steer the kite and gain full control over it before venturing into the waves. Experience suggests that this is best done on a twintip.

The basics[4] illustrated in our first book, *Kitesurfing: The Complete Guide*,[5] are the fundamental principles that should be learned at the start of kitesurfing in the waves. Learning small jumps[6] in particular makes it possible to satisfy the most important requirement, namely learning to control the kite. For this reason we recommend that even beginners coming from a surfing background switch to a twintip board. They can go back to the surfboard once they've learned to control the kite. This method has proved its worth not just for learning quickly, but also when it comes to safety issues.

Previous experience

In addition to the prerequisite of "kitesurfing", as in most sports, there are other aspects of previous experience that make it easier to learn the new sport. We'll take a look now at what these aspects are and how they facilitate the transition to kitesurfing in the waves, as well as why people choose this outdoor sport in particular. "Kiting waves is becoming more and more common and in some parts of the world people start kiting on surfboards now in order to get into the wave," says surfer Sky Solbach, describing how he got into the sport,

namely by using the kite to get into the wave. Watching surfers like Sky when they are kitesurfing in the waves leads us to the conclusion that surfers bring possibly the most useful skills to this new sport, because they can draw on a broad range of experience in relation to waves. Their balancing ability is also developed to an advanced level thanks to surfing, and so the kite, which pulls upwards, tends to increase their stability on the board. They "merely" have to learn how to steer the kite and adapt this to their surf riding, and it soon becomes evident what excellent support this offers when riding waves. Windsurfers with wave experience also have excellent credentials for kitesurfing in the waves. They are quickly able to apply their knowledge of the interaction of wind and waves to the new sport. It is only at the beginning that they might have difficulty in converting the very direct effect of any movement with their rig to a more delayed reaction of the kite on the wave.

Pure freestyle kiters with no experience of waves must first get used to the interaction between the propulsion generated by the kite and the thrust of the wave, and learn to "read the wave". They should approach their first experience of waves in a very structured manner and initially select suitably small waves with onshore conditions. This is because, within these two disciplines, there are not many corresponding manoeuvres which make it easy to learn this new style of riding.

"Regular" or "goofy"?

This relates to whether a person is naturally right- or left-footed, and therefore which foot is placed at the front of the board in surfing or in other sports such as skateboarding. Those who already surf or skateboard don't need to ask themselves this question. Anyone who doesn't know whether they ride with their left foot forward, thus in the regular stance, or with their right, i.e. goofy, should find this out before their first kitesurfing

---

[3] Micky Muñoz, big wave rider: Everything flows.

[4] *Kitesurfing: The Complete Guide*, pp. 30–55.
[5] See Bibliography.
[6] *Kitesurfing: The Complete Guide*, pp. 56–61.

session. Experience shows that it's easier to make the first attempts at riding waves to leeward frontside, i.e. facing the wave and with the natural front foot in the riding direction. Looking towards the water from the beach, this means starting with the wind from the right for regulars, and from the left for goofies.[7] To prevent a "best side" forming, however, and to speed up the learning process – because practising on both sides has been proven not only to accelerate learning, but also to improve stability and variability on the better side – you should also practise riding on the "second-best" side after gaining some initial experience. This is because every wave kiter should master both sides in the long run, although it doesn't mean that every surfer, whether using a sail, a kite or neither, won't prefer one side to the other, just as two-footed football players always have one foot that is stronger.

For all wave kiters, whether regular or goofy, with or without applicable previous experience, the natural prerequisites of wind and waves are the same. It's just that they should be utilized differently depending on one's experience and stance on the board.

Wind and waves

You can obtain information on prevailing wind and wave conditions from websites on the Internet, of course. Nevertheless, some meteorological knowledge is useful so you can assess the general weather situation and seek out wind and wave conditions that match your level of ability, in order to be "in the right place at the right time". Accordingly, we set out below the principles in relation to general weather situations, and to weather conditions suitable for kitesurfing in the waves.

Waves are created by wind. Since both are required for this sport, it's a perfect match. This is only true to a limited extent, however. Although this is the only

[7] See the section on "Choice of location" for this.

Large low-pressure system centred over Iceland.

11

combination we are familiar with in the northern parts of Europe, unfortunately there are only a few days in the year here when the waves are "clean". Waves are only clean when they have travelled a long way across the ocean. And the longer this passage across the ocean, the more ordered the manner in which they hit the shore, which is desirable for good wave riding.

Since the British Isles lie directly off the North Sea coast limiting the "fetch"[8] on which the wind can have an impact, we have to be satisfied here with less spectacular wave conditions. Brilliant wave conditions can be found in locations like Hawaii, Brazil, Australia, South Africa, etc.,[9] where nothing stands in the way of waves that have travelled thousands of miles across the oceans.

Ideally, wave kiters need two wind systems that are independent of one another, but are nevertheless complementary: one that produces the waves and should therefore be far away from the stretch of coastline on which the waves are ridden, and one locally, so as to be able to use the kite.

Admittedly, the relevant websites now relieve all water sports enthusiasts of the job of reading and interpreting weather maps. Nevertheless, a good grasp of the natural conditions that we utilize is helpful if we are to ride the ocean better and above all more safely.

So how does the wind arise? And in particular, how are good waves generated?

Wind

In addition to the explanations about weather given in our book *Kitesurfing: The Complete Guide*,[10] the key points with regard to how the wind arises are described below. This basic knowledge is also essential for understanding how waves are created and being able to

8 Surface area of the sea on which wind generates waves.
9 See section on "Choice of location", p. 16.
10 See Part I, pp. 8–11.

produce a surf forecast on the basis of meteorological conditions.

Wind arises as a result of differences in pressure. These in turn are caused by temperature differences in the atmosphere due to the different rates at which water and land masses heat up. This phenomenon is intensified by the tilt of the earth's axis, which changes the angle at which solar radiation strikes the different parts of the earth's surface during the year it takes for the earth to orbit the sun. The result is a sharp variation in temperature, giving rise to the different seasons that we experience. The Coriolis force produced by the rotation of the earth sets the pressure systems created in motion: in the northern hemisphere, low-pressure areas rotate counter-clockwise, while in the southern hemisphere it is the other way around. Conversely, high-pressure areas spin counter-clockwise in the southern hemisphere and clockwise in the northern hemisphere. Between the typical low-pressure zones created by west winds lie the trade wind belts, extending to the north and south of the equator roughly as far as the 30° line of latitude. In between these belts is the so-called equatorial trough, which is created by the air around the equator heating up and rising. Since the Coriolis force has no effect in this narrow zone around the equator, i.e. the rising air does not circulate, extremely calm conditions, the doldrums, are to be found here for the most part. The air rising here travels north and south at high altitude and cools down. By the time it reaches the respective 30° latitude, it has cooled to the extent that it subsides again and returns in the direction of the equator. The sinking of this cold air creates a high air pressure, and on account of the Coriolis force that prevails in these regions, the high-pressure areas formed cause the wind to be deflected. This gives rise to the typical north-east trade wind in the northern hemisphere and the likewise typical,

reliable south-east trade wind in the southern hemisphere. The trade wind belts shift with the seasons, moving north in the northern hemisphere during the summer months and south in the winter. This migration is not so great, however, that we can benefit from it much in Europe, with the exception of the Canary Isles. Other patterns determine the wind conditions here.

In the west wind zones in these latitudes, from roughly 30° to 60° north, the warm, rising air flowing north is deflected to the right by the aforementioned Coriolis force. Cold air masses originating in the polar regions counteract this air. The ascending warm air masses cause low-pressure areas, while the sinking cold air masses are responsible for high-pressure areas. If a low-pressure area, which can be generated purely thermally, as on the Iberian Peninsula, lies to the east of a high-pressure area, these two areas can exert their effect jointly. This is because the high-pressure system rotates clockwise in the northern hemisphere and the low-pressure system rotates counter-clockwise, due to the fact that the force flowing towards the centre of the low doesn't reach it directly, but is deflected by the earth's rotation (Coriolis effect). The dynamic low-pressure systems prevailing in Europe present a far more typical case, however;

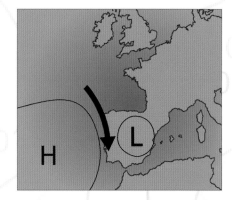

Typical weather pattern for the Galician and Portuguese west coast in the summer months.

12

triggered by the jet stream, which attracts air and thus causes a low to form, the low-pressure areas are set in rapid rotation when the warm air coming from the south meets the cold air arriving from the north. Here a warm front precedes a cold front. Until the faster-moving cold air has overtaken the slower warm air, days often occur on which rotation around the core of the low pressure increases, and with it also the wind speed. In and ahead of warm fronts, which are heralded by layered rain clouds and in which the prevailing wind direction is south-west, the weather is often very squally. Strong showery gusts frequently cause dramatic variations in the wind strength in a matter of seconds. In the warm sector, there's a temporary calm in the weather and the squally conditions abate until the cold front arrives. With a cold front, the approaching cold air pushes under the warm air, forcing the latter up over it – this type of front is recognizable from the dark, vertical cloud formations – and heavy rain follows, accompanied by changeable, strong winds mostly from the west to north-west. Thunderstorms can also occur. Although they give rise to considerable winds, such weather conditions are not universally suitable for kitesurfing in the waves. It is advisable to wait for the fronts to pass, as the wind is then weaker but more constant.

To obtain more constant wind conditions generally, the trade wind belts described above are recommended; but since the trade wind itself does not produce the kind of waves desirable for kitesurfing in the waves, powerful low-pressure systems located some distance away are still a necessity.

And low-pressure systems are always powerful when they exhibit low pressure characteristics, i.e. the air is sucked in rapidly, causing them to spin fast. If the storm blows for long enough and over a large area of ocean, it produces big waves. How this mechanism works in practice is outlined below.

Waves

Wind produces waves – that's no surprise. Equally unspectacular is the fact that in strong wind, small waves can even be created on lakes. This shows the scale the effect of the wind can have on surface conditions. First small capillary waves are formed, which provide a greater contact surface for the wind. They quickly reach a size that prevents the sea surface from being restored and smoothed by surface tension. Gravitational force then causes the waves to start swashing. As the contact surface increases in size, the waves become larger, producing so-called "wind swell". Above a certain wind strength of over 50 knots, wave height no longer increases, because the storm-force wind literally "tears off" the top part of the wave. Accordingly, wind strength is only critical to a limited extent for wave height.

Two other factors exert a significant influence on wave height. As the length of time for which the wind blows on the ocean surface increases, the swell becomes higher and more constant, as the waves become better ordered over time. The fetch mentioned earlier, i.e. the area of water over which the wind has blown, is also a decisive factor. The greater the storm area, the more extended the ocean surface on which the strong wind can achieve the effect described above. The waves travel in the direction of the storm and are continuously charged with energy in the same direction over hundreds of nautical miles. Although this energy may lessen eventually as the wind abates, the energy built up over several hours and a great distance is retained. The rather disordered wind swell with its pointed waves becomes more ordered as the duration of its "journey" increases, producing a uniform, round swell. This is what surfers all over the globe wait for. And the further away they are from its point of origin, the greater their entirely justified hopes of a "clean swell" are, because the greater distance means that the waves become increasingly well

ordered. Why they then arrive on the shore in so-called "sets" will probably remain one of the ocean's secrets.

The swell arrives somewhere on the shore and, depending on the nature of the latter, gives rise to different conditions. Regardless of the character of the coastline, a wave advances in the form of orbital movements that extend to a depth equivalent to half the wavelength (distance between wave crests). It's not the water that is being swept towards the shore, but the energy imparted to the water by the wind. If the depth of water close to the shore is no longer sufficient to give free rein to this transfer of energy, the lower part of the wave is braked by the subsurface. The upper part of the wave carries on moving towards the shore, where it breaks.

Here the composition of the seabed close to the shore is responsible for how the wave breaks – slowly, from top to bottom, or in a steep and hollow manner. For riding the surf, this calls for different skills; or looked at from another angle, it opens up a variety of possibilities.

A gently sloping sandy seabed, such as those found on many northern European beaches, causes the wave crest to curl forward slowly so that the wave pushes white water ahead of it and increasingly loses height as it approaches the shore. These conditions are well suited to beginners taking up the sport of kitesurfing in the waves.

Not every beach break is the same, however. There are many beaches on which sandbanks pose a sudden obstacle to the lower part of the wave. The most spectacular examples of this type of beach break are probably La Gravière in France, Mudaka in Spain and Puerto Escondido on Mexico's mainland. Here the lower part of the wave is braked suddenly on the sandbank. Compression of the wave pushes the wave crest upwards, not only increasing the height of the wave but also sending it crashing heavily into the wave trough from above.

This creates conditions for fast wave

13

Waves breaking in a typical beach break with a gently shelving subsurface.

The waves break in a steep, hollow manner on a reef break or on a beach break with a steeply sloping subsurface.

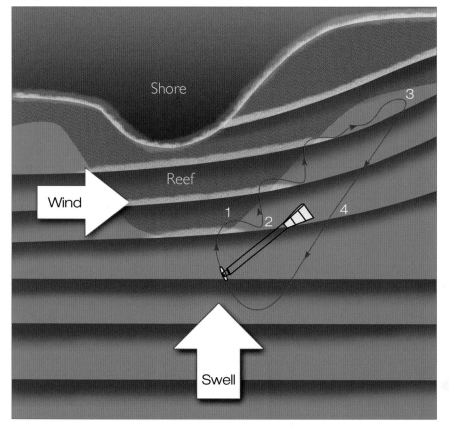

Down the line at a pointbreak: the perfect conditions.
1 – bottom turn, 2 – top turn, 3 – jibe, 4 – go upwind back to point.

14

riding with dynamic manoeuvres on and above the lip of the wave. A very similar situation arises in the case of so-called reef breaks. Here, however, the sharply rising subsurface is formed not by a sandbank but by a reef. If the reef sticks out into the sea at a favourable angle to the swell direction under the surface of the water, the waves start breaking at a defined point and continue to "peel" and break along the edge of the reef. This is called a pointbreak and probably offers the best conditions for experienced wave kiters if the wind and its direction are right.

In addition to the superb opportunities for surfing a wave to leeward, a pointbreak typically allows you to kite back upwind to the top of the point around the back of the impact zone without having to kite directly through the line-up.

Be warned, however! Inexperienced wave kiters should generally exercise caution at a reef break, as mistakes are less easily forgiven than in slowly breaking waves. Anyone experiencing their first wipe-out in the surf across the reef, which can be a painful enough occurrence depending on the composition of the reef, might be held underwater for quite some time. The situation can be even worse with a dropped kite. And so this is another reminder of the importance of choosing a kiting location suited to one's level of ability.[11] We advise beginners to practise in principle in beach breaks.

Weather patterns suitable for kitesurfing in the waves

In northern Europe or on other coastlines where the wind and waves are generated by the same system, it's advisable not to go out as soon as the wind picks up; be patient and wait a while, as the waves will improve over time. In addition, as mentioned above, the time after the front has passed through is better for kiting and

[11] See section on "Choice of location" (p. 16).

above all safer due to the more constant wind conditions. With reference to the low-pressure system illustrated here, this means the following:

With the arrival of the warm front, the south-west wind increases sharply and is very squally. The waves created are initially very small and choppy. It is therefore recommended to wait for the front to pass through, as the wind will then abate somewhat and turn more westerly. Although the waves will quickly diminish in size, they will be more regular. Given a choice, it's worth waiting for the cold front to pass too, as this brings stronger wind and higher waves. The wind direction is north-west, which produces good sideshore conditions on many beaches in northern Europe. Apart from the more constant wind conditions, what encourages many kiters to wait for the weather following behind the fronts is the fact that the sun also reappears.

If the waves to be ridden are the result of a distant storm, then it's a good idea to go out on the water as soon as the swell arrives. This is because larger waves travel faster across the ocean and hit the coast sooner. A weather pattern offering conditions of this kind can be seen on the weather map reproduced here.

For good conditions on the west coast of Portugal, in Morocco or in the Canary Isles, a deep low over the Atlantic is desirable, setting a swell in motion towards the south. The local weather conditions then provide the corresponding wind. In Portugal this is the low that is produced by the heat over the Iberian Peninsula and causes a north-south flow together with the Atlantic high. This can be amplified by local geographical conditions. It's a similar situation in Morocco, where the effect of the Atlantic high is strengthened by the African heat low.

The basic system driving the weather in both Morocco and the Canary Isles as well as further south in the Cape Verde Islands is the north-east trade wind. On the coast of Portugal and Morocco, this

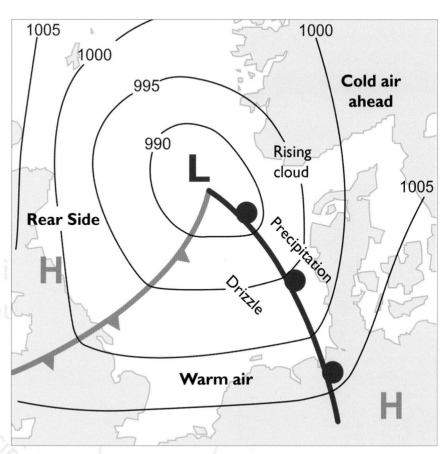

Typical low-pressure system with a warm front and a following cold front in northern Europe (in diagram form).

weather pattern, described above, gives rise to sideshore conditions with wind from the right. Those preferring wind from the left should look instead to the Canary Isles, e.g. El Medano, or since this pattern also produces the Levante which blows from the east, to Caños de Meca at Cape Trafalgar.

For the virtually limitless list of spots in the southern hemisphere, the picture is similar but reversed, because the Coriolis force means that lows and highs rotate in the opposite direction – a low-pressure system spins clockwise and a high-pressure system counter-clockwise. Take an example from Western Australia: a well-developed low-pressure area above the Indian Ocean sends a powerful swell in the direction of the coast of Western

Australia. Sucked in by the thermal low over the great Australian desert, the fresher sea air is deflected northwards and supported by the local high. This wind has become known as the "Fremantle Doctor" after the port of Fremantle, which hosted the Americas Cup. This wind system travels along the entire Western Australian coast and, in conjunction with the swell created, it produces terrific conditions for kitesurfing in the waves with a sideshore wind from the left, especially in Gnaraloo, north of Carnarvon.

A similar phenomenon in South Africa, where the wind announces its arrival spectacularly with the formation of the "table cloth" over Table Mountain, is called the "Cape Doctor". Along the west coast there, heading north from

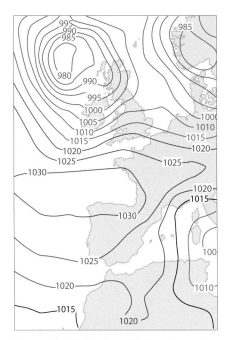

Pressure distribution in an ideal weather system for surfing on the west coast of Portugal and for kitesurfing in the waves on the Atlantic coast of Morocco and the Canary Isles.

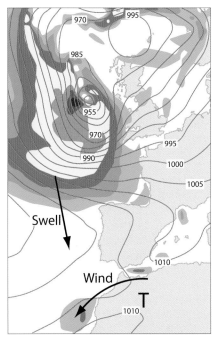

Storm region and the swell direction triggered by the low-pressure area.

Platboom Bay on the Cape of Good Hope, are many good kitesurfing spots with wind from the left. These are mostly beach breaks at which the wind decreases as one gets further away from the metropolis of Capetown. In Elandsbaii, a small place on the west coast of South Africa, the waves break cleanly over a reef, offering superb conditions for surfers and wave kiters.

Conclusion: In summary, it should be said that in northern Europe we often have to make do with a single weather system supplying the wind and waves. This frequently brings gusty winds, waves that are not so "clean" and bad weather. If thermal wind conditions are to provide steady propulsion for the kite, then head for latitudes in which high-pressure areas interacting with thermal lows provide the wind. For good waves, strong low-pressure systems as far away as possible are required. These systems should occur regularly according to the season.

Choice of location

Great conditions for kitesurfing in the waves can be found all over the globe. There are a few factors to take into account however, when planning your next kitesurfing session or holiday. First, and most important, is your skill level. Know your limits and choose small waves and/or onshore wind initially before heading out into bigger waves. Other points to consider are your preference of wave type and riding direction and also weather patterns. We cannot possibly cover every kitesurfing spot below, but we can nonetheless suggest a few good examples.

■ Possibly the world's most legendary kitesurfing wave spot is **Maui, Hawaii.** Situated in the middle of the Pacific Ocean, Maui is a target for big swell from every direction, especially in winter. Although not the most consistent or predictable time for wind,

the winter months nonetheless offer the best opportunity to ride big waves. The trade winds are at their strongest and most consistent during the summer months, from May to August, although the waves are typically much smaller then. The best time to catch both wind and waves in Hawaii is during spring and fall. Lanes on Maui's north shore offers great but challenging conditions, while Kanaha and Spreckelsville, also on the north shore, are better suited for intermediate kitesurfers, as these spots are not so exposed to the swell. However, it is worth keeping in mind that all wave spots on Maui can become dangerously big during any season, so be cautious.

■ The wind also blows from the right on the west coast of the Iberian Peninsula. In **Galicia** there are spots where days of big waves are not uncommon. Unfortunately there is often no wind here, or it is too weak. This problem does not tend to arise in **Portugal's** most well-known surf spot, **Guincho.** The wind here, which blows from the north at the edge of the Iberian heat low, is amplified by local thermals. In most cases, its interaction with an Atlantic swell produces demanding kitesurfing conditions: on the one hand, the wind tends to be very strong, while on the other the waves become very powerful and often break quite heavily. Good conditions are most likely to occur here in the summer months.

■ **Baja California, Mexico:** It's worth making the long journey that takes you initially through Tijuana and Ensenada and then south through desert-like regions, because this long coastline offers something to suit every taste and level of ability. For newcomers to kitesurfing in the waves, the eastern side of the peninsula, far to the south at La Ventana and Cabo Pulmo, offers good opportunities in the winter months to learn the basics with wind from the left. If you want to stay longer and master the sport properly, terrific conditions can be found at the pointbreaks in Punta Abreojos and Punta San Carlos from mid-April to mid-October. Although good waves are only formed with a southerly swell at Punta Abreojos, at Punta San Carlos the northerly swell also provides optimum conditions. But beware – getting in and out of the water is not without its hazards at either spot, on account of the reef formation, and so these locations are only recommended for very experienced wave kiters! Beach breaks with wind from the right can be found on the Pacific side north of Cabo San Lucas, but often the wind isn't strong enough here.

■ **Australia**: The fifth continent is always worth a visit. If you want to avoid the surfing masses on the east coast, especially around Surfers Paradise, the west coast is a pretty good alternative. From October to February, the "Fremantle Doctor", a wind produced by a thermal low above the great Australian desert, blows frequently there. In conjunction with the swells occurring in the Indian Ocean, this wind offers terrific opportunities for kitesurfing in the waves with wind from the left along the entire coast.

■ A good venue for novices is **Tarifa**, especially when the Poniente is blowing. This side-onshore wind blows from the right and the waves are rarely too big to surf. If, as often happens, the Levante blows strongly from the east, Tarifa becomes unsuitable for kitesurfing in the waves – partly because there are no good waves and partly because the wind is offshore and is frequently too strong and gusty as far up as Punta Paloma. The closest location for escaping this is **Bolonia**, where the conditions can be quite different. If the wind is too strong there as well, this is a good sign that

favourable conditions can be found in **Caños de Meca**. At the famous Cape Trafalgar, the wind blowing from the left makes it possible to surf waves right into the bay, but it's important to look out for the rocks below the surface; they may aid good wave formation, but can be dangerous at low tide, especially when entering and exiting the water. If the weather conditions remain stable over several days, the Levante can become too strong even in Caños; then it's advisable to head further west. On days like this, good conditions can be found at **Novo Sancti Petri** with its long, sandy beach.

■ In the **Canaries** there are many good spots where wave height, the type of break and wind conditions vary. On the north coast of **Fuerteventura** are several very well-known wave spots, but they are not recommended for beginners on some days. On **Lanzarote**, the bay of Famara offers good conditions for novices as well as stunning surroundings. A list of surf spots in the Canaries would fill several pages, but we'll cut this one short here. Suffice it to say that the most reliable season for wind in the Canaries is the summer, when the NE trade blows pretty consistently. The

prospect of good waves, however, is much better in the winter months thanks to the North Atlantic lows.

■ **South Africa** sometimes offers perfect conditions during the winter months in the northern hemisphere. The prospect of really good kitesurfing conditions is best around Cape Town, where Sunset Beach, Table View and Blueberg are relatively close by. When the Cape Doctor blows, these beaches close to the city are the first to feel the wind. However, if the wind there is too strong for your liking, you can escape west, first to Melkbos and Yserfontain, then to Elandsbai, where a pointbreak with wind from the left creates perfect conditions. Just as on the east coast, there are plenty of other spots here too, some of which are ideal for kitesurfing in the waves.

■ **France's Atlantic coast** is well known for its excellent waves, even in the summer months. Unfortunately, the wind is often not strong enough; the further south you travel, the better the waves, but the smaller the chance of good wind, which is created here by an afternoon thermal. On **France's Mediterranean shoreline**, as on **Sardinia** and **Corsica**, waves build up

17

when the Mistral blows. Similarly strong but less spectacular in terms of wave formation is the Tramontane. Both winds are created by the interaction of a high-pressure area over northern Spain and south-west France with a low-pressure area over northern Italy. This configuration of a high-pressure system rotating clockwise and the low-pressure system rotating counter-clockwise draws in air masses from the north. When these masses flow along a line from Bordeaux to Perpignan, the Tramontane is produced, which blows from west-north-west over the western part of the Gulf of Lion. Due to the wind direction, the waves generated tend to be less surfable. If these air masses travel a path from Lyon to Marseille, they are accelerated down the Rhône Valley and often attain storm force by the time they reach the Mediterranean. Now and then large waves are created that can be surfed on various beaches in the eastern part of the **Gulf of Lion**. The wind blows from the right and is often very strong, enabling you to use small kites. This weather pattern can occur all year round, but is more likely to be seen during the winter months.

■ Also ideal for kitesurfing in the waves are the **Oregon coast** and **northern California** on the West Coast of the USA. In the summer months, a north wind often blows, which can be used for kitesurfing on many beaches along a stretch of coastline extending for hundreds of miles, because the Pacific generates an almost endless supply of waves. Heading north out of San Francisco on the wonderful Pacific Coast Highway (State Route 1), you pass several good spots: Pistol River, the South Jetty of Florence, Newport, and so on.

■ Going south from San Francisco, apart from the many beautiful stretches of

coastline, there are also plenty of good kitesurfing beaches along this section of the **Californian coast**. Wadell Creek and Davenport are just two examples of beaches where the wind blows from the right in the summer months and there's almost always a good Pacific swell. Further south, the winds to the north of the Los Angeles metropolis are much poorer. Anyone who is seeking good reef breaks and doesn't mind remote, lonely beaches should venture on past San Diego to the start of the 1000-mile long coast of Baja California in Mexico.

■ For a long time, **Morocco** was regarded as "somewhere a bit different", with perfect waves well away from overcrowded beaches, and was only sought out by a handful of surfers worldwide. Then increasing numbers of windsurfers began to congregate there in the summer months, and now wave kiters too. There's a good reason for this: with a coastline extending over 2500 kilometres, Morocco offers optimum conditions for kitesurfing in the waves at all levels of ability, with a high probability of wind. But pack very small kites if you're travelling to the windy region around the beautiful port of Essaouira!

■ Northern **Brazil** is renowned for its many beach breaks. With sideshore wind from the right, these are great for beginners. The best waves, though, tend to be in the south, in Rio and beyond, although the wind isn't as constant. From August to December the wind is strong and very consistent.

■ **The North Sea coast of Denmark** offers very good conditions for kitesurfing in the waves, but like the North Sea coast of Germany it's heavily dependent on low-pressure

systems bringing waves. Nevertheless, various options exist: in the north-west, the best conditions with wind from the right are to be found in **Hvide Sande** south of the harbour mole. Those who prefer wind from the left can enjoy good conditions at **Hanstholm**. **Klitmøller** is ideal for kiting with west and south-west wind.

■ Along the southwest coast of England, **Cornwall** and **Devon**, along with **southern Wales**, are ideal British kitesurfing spots, due to their tendency to pick up the swell and also because of the pleasant water temperature brought up from the south by the Gulf Stream. A variety of weather patterns in this region creates good kitesurfing conditions along different parts of the coastline. For example, the combination of a high over the British Isles and a low over France produces an easterly wind in Bigbury Bay, east of Plymouth, which is great for kitesurfing in the waves, particularly with wind from the left if there is a good swell running through the wide open bay. Southwest or west wind caused by a low, west of Britain and a high over Europe brings wind from the right to K-Bay (Kimmeridge Bay), near Bournemouth, providing great riding conditions. Cornwall's most popular spot, Watergate Bay, also works well in a southwest wind. However, for 2 hours before and 2 hours after high tide, it is not accessible to kiters as the beach is submerged, leaving only the cliffs. For those with time to travel further north from Watergate Bay, however, many other good kitesurfing spots can be found.

As we've said already, we don't claim to offer a complete list of locations here. Besides, seeking out your favourite spot for kitesurfing in the waves is all part of enjoying the experience of this outdoor sport.

2 Safety

"Why do people devote their entire life to riding a wave on a board?" asks Stacy Peralta, the producer of "Riding Giants" – and rightly so, because surfing large and powerful waves always entails a degree of danger. The answer lies in the quest for an experience in which the rider forgets everything going on around him, because the external demands made on him match perfectly with his individual abilities. And this point at the limit of one's individual skills always carries an element of risk. Csikszentmihalyi[12] calls the resulting, desirable state "flow". As one's ability improves, however, the conditions that must be sought to trigger the flow experience become increasingly exacting, because the lack of challenge presented by always kiting in the same, and therefore less demanding, conditions no longer gives rise to this flow state. But the more demanding the spot chosen by the surfer, the more dangerous it is also. One should bear in mind here that overchallenging oneself by seeking out unsuitable conditions – in this case conditions that are too difficult – is no better for triggering the sense of elation that the flow experience brings. Anyone surfing in waves that are too big and powerful for their level of skill will not only miss out on the terrific flow sensation, when time and space become one, but will also put themselves and perhaps others too in danger. In addition, conditions that are too difficult and hazardous prompt feelings of anxiety, and anxiety is a bad companion, not only because it stops one from learning successfully, but also because it blocks the flow experience. You also miss out on the additional energy that the motivation generated by flow brings with it. Motivation research has long shown that the requirements of a chosen task should neither be too great nor too small if the optimum energy is to be created and the best learning results achieved.

In addition to choosing the most suitable conditions for his level of ability, it is essential that a kiter can and should reduce risk levels to a personal minimum by adopting the safety measures outlined below:

1. On the basis of the above, it is important to exercise great care in your **choice of location**. This means that the spot chosen must suit your skill level. Consideration should be given both to the seasonal wind and wave conditions, and to tidal currents. If wind and current are coming from the same direction, particular attention should be paid to ensuring that going upwind does not pose any problems and that you can get back to the point from which you started. If there is any doubt about this, you must ensure that adequate opportunities exist for landing safely to leeward. The height of the waves and the manner in which they break are also of crucial importance. With a pronounced shorebreak, the beach start must be reliably mastered, i.e. its swift execution should not pose any problems. If you haven't fully grasped the timing and the turning motion of riding waves, don't seek out spots where the waves break fast and hollow, but first acquire the required riding techniques in slower, crumbly waves. This is an appeal to every wave kiter to make a realistic assessment of the conditions and preferably to observe the waves once more from the beach instead of taking too great a risk.

2. Kiting in **consistent wind conditions** is not only more fun, but less hazardous. This has already been proven by a wide-ranging study, from which it clearly emerged that the accident rate in spots with sharply varying wind conditions due to fronts was significantly higher than in locations where consistent wind conditions prevailed. The severity of injuries also increases in locations where wind conditions are inconsistent. It can be concluded from this that when kiting in northern Europe, where the wind systems are created by low-pressure areas, the fronts should be observed very carefully. This is because extremely changeable wind conditions normally prevail ahead of and in the warm and cold fronts, and these can pose a danger. It is recommended to let the fronts pass and to take advantage of the classic weather following behind them for kitesurfing in the waves. Of course, this doesn't mean that the weather situation shouldn't be carefully monitored in all other spots too!

3. When **setting up** the kite, the same level of caution is advised as when carrying out the **gear check** before starting. When inflating the kite, you need to hold on to it with your free hand or attach it to the pump leash and then weight it down with sand once it is laid down. You should always attach the lines yourself following the manufacturer's instructions. The attachment points of the lines to the bar and the kite must be checked before every launch, to exclude as far as possible the danger of a line breaking at sea.

4. Many kiting spots are situated at the foot of cliffs or on rock-strewn coastlines. Here the **launch** needs to be thought through more carefully than on sandy beaches. Special attention needs to be paid to leeward, which must be free of obstructions and any passers-by.

5. You <u>must</u> know the **international kiting**

---

12 1999, p. 62.

signs for "Help", "Okay to launch", "Abort launch" and "Landing the kite":

Help.

Okay to launch.

Abort launch.

Landing the kite.

6. You must be able to use the **quick release** reliably. If something unforeseen should happen, the decision to operate the quick release must be taken and executed quickly. Depending on the wave height, it can be highly expedient to operate the quick release immediately if the kite is "dropped" in front of a big wave and it's clear that it cannot be launched again promptly before the wave breaks. If a fairly large wave breaks into a kite with the rider still hooked in, it can pull him so quickly that he gets dragged underwater, making it difficult for him to resurface. The kite can also tear more easily due to greater resistance to the wave with the weight of the kiter attached to it.

7. In addition to the **general "rules of the road"**:

- ◼ "Vessel with the wind from port gives way to the vessel with the wind from the starboard side"
- ◼ "Leeward before windward"
- ◼ "Overtaking vessels keep clear"
- ◼ "An upwind kiter on the same course as a downwind kiter steers his kite high and the downwind rider flies his kite low"
- ◼ "Last-minute manoeuvre"[13]

there are surf-specific **right-of-way rules** in surf spots. Kiters are urged to observe these both for safety reasons and for reasons of fairness and mutual respect:

- ◼ If two surfers – regardless of whether they are surfers, windsurfers or kitesurfers – are on the same wave, the rider who was on the wave first may ride the wave. If this is not clear, the rider who is closer to the breaking part of the wave, the curl, has right of way.
- ◼ When kiting out into the line-up, the general rule accepted worldwide is to

---

[13] Covered in greater detail in *Kitesurfing: The Complete Guide*, p. 14.

keep out of the way of any incoming surfer, kitesurfer or windsurfer riding a wave. This is only possible by maintaining enough distance, because wave rides using a kite take up a lot of space to leeward because of the length of the lines. If meeting halfway should nevertheless be unavoidable, the applicable rule is that the surfer on the wave must give way to the surfer who is riding or paddling out, as he has greater manoeuvrability due to the push and speed of the wave.

8. Carrying out a **warm-up session**[14] helps protect the kiter from injury and also from the onset of fatigue, which can give rise to hazardous situations out on the ocean. A good **level of fitness**, which can be achieved or maintained by exercises ashore to complement the kitesurfing training sessions on the water, is also important for this.

9. Using **mental imaging**[15] lends greater reliability to sequences of movement. This helps in learning tricks more quickly and in reducing the danger posed by failed attempts at tricks. In addition, by increasing the reliability of the sequence, mental imaging minimizes anxiety, especially in relation to very demanding conditions at the upper limits of the rider's ability. This in turn renders the surfer more capable of acting, even in hazardous situations.

10. Wearing a helmet is especially recommended, as in the event of a wipe-out in front of a wave, the wave can easily catch the board, which could then hit the kiter's head. A head injury incurred in this way can be life-threatening if there is a temporary loss of consciousness in the water.

11. Kitesurfing in waves is best

---

[14] See section on "General training recommendations", p. 22.
[15] See section on "Mental imaging", p. 25.

undertaken **without a leash**, as this can jeopardize the rider's safety.

12. Your ability to **self-rescue** increases your safety! Self-rescue in waves is heavily dependent on the conditions and the position of the kiter, and must ultimately be judged according to the situation. The first priority is that the wave kiter should never in principle let go of his board in order to swim to the shore. If he should get into serious trouble outside the break, for example because a line snaps, he must be able to rescue himself, as there isn't always a rescue boat around. The decision regarding self-rescue should be taken in good time, i.e. as soon as the kiter becomes aware of the emergency. If a kiter is familiar with self-rescue from training, it's easier for him to make the decision at the right time than if he is uncertain of the procedure. The opportunity must be taken while self-rescue is still possible. Once the kiter has unhooked himself, he must pull the kite towards him and turn it onto its back. If necessary he can swim back to shore like this, holding the kite by the leading edge. Breaking waves should be avoided while doing this. If the wind is side-onshore the kite can also be used as a sail to pull the kiter ashore. Letting a little air out of the front tube makes this easier and allows the kiter to pull both tips towards him and hold them such that the kite fills with wind to some extent. To "sail" back to the shore in this manner, the kiter can lie on his board.

If this means of self-rescue doesn't work and the land recedes further into the distance, it may be necessary to part with the kite and paddle ashore lying on the board. In this case, however, it should be carefully considered whether this is actually possible, because if the rider were to be driven further out to sea, it would be highly sensible to hold onto the kite – on the one hand because it's a good buoyancy aid and on the other because it's easily visible from the air, for example from a helicopter. There's no

patent remedy for such situations: the right decision always depends on a number of factors, namely the wave height, wind, current, time of day, temperature, and the rider's physical condition and personal approach to handling such emergency situations. To enable him to make a good decision according to the circumstances, the rider should analyse the situation briefly yet thoroughly.

In an emergency inside the break, it's advisable depending on the wave height and the nature of the ocean bed to part with one's kite and paddle back to shore on the board.

As a basic principle, you should practise the emergency response, because this reduces the fear of emergency situations to a minimum and as such contributes to a trouble-free kitesurfing experience.

13. Never go kiting alone!

21

3 Tips on training

Taking general and specific training tips into consideration helps speed up the learning process. These training tips relate to a long-term training strategy and provide pointers for putting together individual training sessions on the water with preparatory mental imaging.

For kitesurfing in the waves, it is also true that carefully planned training sessions, which build on one another, minimize the risks posed by an extreme sport such as this. Targeted training reduces the frequency of accidents, which is necessary if our sport is to grow. Therefore, in addition to the advice given in previous chapters, we have included some specific training tips in the following section.

General tips on training

If you wish to learn successfully, i.e. to make rapid, far-reaching and safe progress, you should proceed in a structured manner, as in freestyle kiting and all other sports.

This means determining the content of a training session, practising it in a concentrated manner during the session, and then reflecting on it afterwards, recognizing unsuitable manoeuvres and any errors, and drawing conclusions for planning future training sessions.

All kitesurfers who can get back to where they started with their board, i.e. are able to go upwind, are generally in a position to gain their first experience of kitesurfing in the waves. But it's essential that they begin in side-onshore conditions with waves roughly at waist height. Due to their speed and power, bigger waves can influence the interaction

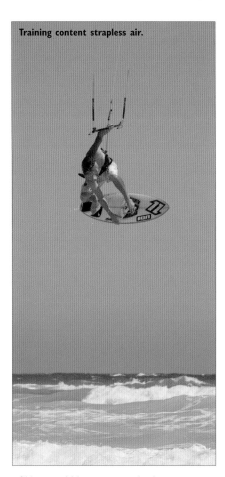

Training content strapless air.

of kiter and kite so strongly that unintentional kite movements upset the balance of forces, leading to severe wipe-outs or dropping of the kite in the wave. Sufficient room should be available to leeward – the direction in which the wave is ridden – and no other surfers should be on the wave.

As is evident from the order of the basics and tricks to be practised in Part II, it is important to structure the long-term training strategy in relation to the choice of suitable locations described above. In

addition to the safety aspects addressed, there are also motivational reasons for this. The level of difficulty of the tasks selected should be neither too high nor too low, in order to facilitate the flow experience and thus achieve good motivation. This is because, as outlined earlier, you only experience the sensation of flow if the conditions match your ability. The feeling you then experience is sufficient motivation to carry on practising and seeking out similar situations time and again. The euphoric state attained when everything – the conditions and your own physical and emotional state – seems to be in harmony is not the sole preserve of every extreme sports enthusiast. But achieving this state is down to the athlete himself; all he needs to do is to choose the right wind and wave conditions, and training content suited to his level of ability.

Long-term training strategy

It has proved extremely useful to practise board and kite control without waves to start with. The aim of this is to experience and practise kite control in relation to board control for the jibe and the bottom turn with regard to the proper timing. This is because the crucial difference in relation to windsurfing lies, as stated above, in the fact that kiting in waves calls for delayed timing. If this isn't correctly coordinated, the kiter would lose board speed or ride underneath the kite, reducing his ability to control the kite or resulting in the kite being dropped. And this is only safe in small waves. Therefore, coordination of kite and board control is an essential element that must be practised. It should be kept in mind here that control of the kite must

22

be exercised depending on the carve radius among other things, which in turn is largely dictated by the wave.

It is recommended to match this timing to the conditions, i.e. a small wave initially. The timing is "internalized" in this way. The critical factor here is that you must be able to constantly fly the kite without looking at it, as you need to watch the wave carefully. When riding the wave to leeward, there is a danger of "riding underneath" the kite, causing it to drop; and a dropped kite can be dangerous in waves, because the wave breaking into the kite can not only destroy the kite but can drag the kiter forcefully under the water. The training tip to be derived from this is to practise small turns with the board while exerting appropriate kite control. This will prevent a loss of tension in the lines.

It goes without saying that the turn must be suited to the waves, which can also mean that, depending on the wave, you must occasionally travel in a very wide carving motion, for example to turn around a close out section or to manoeuvre yourself via a long drawn-out carve precisely into the steepest part of the wave.

Conclusion: Kitesurfing in the waves is a complex sport, in which one's actions must be very closely coordinated with the given conditions. To achieve this, basic skills like board control and the corresponding kite control adapted to the situation and the waves are best learned in easy conditions. This means that the wind–wave configuration chosen must be suitable for the manoeuvres to be learned in the session, and that some of the basics should first be practised on flat water. The recommended order for learning the basics and the tricks based on these corresponds to the sequence of basics, manoeuvres and tricks shown in Part II, "Training on the water".

23

Short-term training strategy and structuring a training unit

The structure of a training unit on the water should always be determined depending on the weather conditions. Once a decision has been made on the content of the training session in accordance with the wind and wave situation, it's a question of visualizing the theoretical knowledge by way of the manoeuvres to be practised. Mental imaging has proved to be a very useful way of accelerating the learning process, and this technique should precede training out on the ocean. Following this comes the warm-up phase, which we seriously recommend. After the session on the water comes the cool-down phase and time to reflect on the training unit.

Warm-up and cool-down

In the world of sport, kitesurfing in the waves is viewed as one of the "fun" sports, but from a purely physiological point of view it should be taken just as seriously as any other sport. And in every other sport, no matter in which league or at what level it's played, participants have a warm-up and cool-down routine. There are good medical and sports science reasons for these routines, which are generally accepted as being essential.

They are earnestly recommended for kitesurfing too, because the continuous strain it imposes on the body gives rise to a higher tonicity, which can quickly lead to fatigue if the body is not prepared for it and also to uneconomical movements and actions that are not in harmony with one another. The constant high level of tonicity prevents the cardiovascular system from delivering the optimum supply of blood to the muscles, because the blood vessels are obstructed in their transport function by ongoing muscle contractions. This fact plays a crucial role in both preparing for the training session and the follow-up to it, and makes the warm-up and cool-down phases indispensable.

Warm-up

An increased level of activity of the cardiovascular system serves primarily to increase the metabolism, i.e. the relevant muscles are supplied with oxygen and nutrients, and by-products such as lactose, generated when the muscles are working in kitesurfing, can be removed more easily. This mechanism is known to function better following a warm-up routine. The same applies especially to the joints, which transmit all the forces occurring. The stresses produced should be rated as pretty high, meaning that joints that are not properly prepared are more susceptible to injury and signs of wear. Sometimes these effects only come to light after years of considerable strain. As well as activating the cardiovascular system, the warm-up leads to an increase in the thickness of cartilage, resulting in a greater take-up of synovial fluid, which improves the joint's buffer function.

In addition to preventing injury and wear and tear, the activation phase increases the conduction rate of the neurons,[16] which improves the capacity for action and thus your performance.

We recommend a loose, ten-minute limbering-up session with exercises to activate the torso and shoulders. To take account of the specific stresses generated when kitesurfing in the waves and to be well prepared for them, it has proved valuable to follow this general session with specific mobilizing exercises. This entails developing one's balancing ability in particular. This should not only be activated for the training session ahead, but should also be exercised independently of it:

1. Standing on one leg, you should try to maintain your balance for as long as possible.

2. Take your arms out of the balance equation by crossing them behind your back.

3. If as a third step you can maintain your balance effortlessly even with your eyes closed, your balance system is sufficiently activated to perform well. The accompanying activation of proprioception,[17] which is recognizable from the balancing adjustments carried out automatically during the exercise, protects against injury.

Therefore, a warm-up routine prior to kitesurfing assists in preparing for a good performance as well as helping to minimize acute injuries and signs of wear.

Cool-down

During training out on the water, a high metabolic rate sets in, which facilitates muscle function in conjunction with the nervous system. It gives rise to by-products resulting from the work done by the muscles and from nerve activity, so-called metabolites, which have to be removed or converted. This calls for sustained activity of the cardiovascular system at a lower level. Consequently, the muscles, which have a high tonicity, often due to the continuous static work they carry out during kitesurfing, must not be "switched off" immediately on landing, but need to be kept going and brought down slowly to a resting state. This is achieved by 5 to 20 minutes of easy jogging plus related loosening-up exercises. The effectiveness of stretching to avoid symptoms of fatigue and aching muscles after exertion has not been proven; nevertheless, it might at least help to reduce a high level of tonicity.

Following the jog, it's vital to top up fluids and energy reserves by taking on board adequate quantities of liquid and carbohydrates.

24

---

[16] Nerve cells.

[17] Proprio = own, + perception.

Mental imaging

As in many other types of sports, mental imaging has already proven to be of great value in freestyle kitesurfing.[18] Tricks can be learned faster and above all more safely with mental preparation. Ultimately "the virtually classic application" of mental imaging is ascribed to "sports with complex, highly coordinated movements that are also geared to precision and short decision-making moments".[19] And in our sport, the movements are highly coordinated, with an emphasis on balancing ability — probably the most notable of the seven coordinative abilities when it comes to kitesurfing in the waves.

In addition, in this extreme sport discipline, the kiter's actions depend on the constantly changing conditions of the wind, and especially the waves, calling in turn for split-second decision making. For kitesurfing, this calls for the application of mental imaging in general, and of two of the known mental imaging methods in particular.

Before we give precise instructions on how to apply these two mental imaging techniques to kitesurfing in the waves, however, a few general observations on mental imaging should be made.

Contrary to the view widely held,

[18] *Kitesurfing: The Complete Guide*, pp. 21–25.

[19] Gabler, Hauser, Hug & Steiner, 1985, p. 235.

25

reducing emotional responses such as anxiety is only a secondary aim of mental imaging. Its main purpose, as the term suggests, is to visualize forthcoming actions. This could be described as playing an "internal film". The origins of this method, which has been applied successfully to sport, lie in behaviour therapy. Mental imaging is "learning and/or improving a movement sequence by means of intensive visualisation without simultaneous realisation of the movement visualised".[20] The aim is to make it simpler to learn a movement in a new sport by creating an image of the movement, or to improve the actual movement by improving the image. In our case, waves that pose a greater potential risk, for example, can be ridden in the surfer's imagination before he ventures out onto the water himself. It could thus be described simply as an "internal rehearsal".[21]

The sequence reliability that is produced by visualization gives the athlete the impression in a real situation that he has already performed this trick or this ride several times previously. This makes it more likely that the trick will succeed. Not only does this make learning easier for beginners, but it also offers professional surfers a wide variety of options with regard to sequence reliability when surfing big waves or refining their techniques.

There are two prerequisites for ensuring that mental imaging achieves the desired effect: on the one hand, the athlete must have a positive attitude towards the method itself, which can be achieved by factual clarification of this training measure. On the other hand, the desired effect is only achieved if the trainee is in "a state of relative relaxation" when performing mental imaging.[22] This is because optimum visualization intensity can only be reached by someone who is in a mentally and physically relaxed state overall. Listening to relaxing music or performing breathing exercises are two possible ways of attaining the necessary state of relaxation.

Visualization

Compared with freestyle kiting, a modified method is recommended for visualizing kitesurfing in the waves. This is because in this sport, the external factors are dictated by the wave and so this defines a temporal and spatial framework for the trick in question. It is essential to take this into account, as harmony can only be achieved by working with the forces of nature and not against them. The accomplished and apparently playful movement of some surfers is the result of extensive experience in waves – experience that manifests itself in the way they are able to shape their actions perfectly to suit the medium and exploit its force and dynamics for their performance. To be able to do this, it is first necessary to fully understand the wave, to recognize its rhythm and to develop an in-depth knowledge of the path it takes. It makes sense to find a spot where you can sit and observe the wave undisturbed, and you should then observe it until you have committed a picture of the wave to mind. You should then familiarize yourself with the objective, i.e. you must decide what you want to practise, depending on the wind and wave conditions prevailing.

The question of what mental imaging should focus on must therefore be answered clearly and should be restricted to one trick. At this point it

[20] Tiwald, 1973, p. 57. Volpert (1977, p. 66) defines mental imaging in a similar manner as "the systematically repeated, deliberate visualisation of a sporting action without its simultaneous practical execution".
[21] Tiwald, 1984, p. 57.

[22] Eberspächer, 1990, p. 76.

The wave "internalized".

makes sense to choose a trick suited to your level of ability and the given conditions – the tricks are shown in detail in Part II "Training on the water" – and to gain an in-depth understanding of this. The photo sequences have been selected so that all the basic elements of a trick can be understood, an essential prerequisite for the success of the mental imaging. The subsequent production of the movement image is the theoretical reproduction of an image of a movement stored in the memory. The perception of the action must be formulated in the athlete's own words. This should reflect the trick's overall complexity and the dynamic, temporal and spatial relationships between the elements of a trick, i.e. the complex ride on the wave observed in real-time or in slow motion. Only then is the ride replayed repeatedly in the mind, with two basic forms of mental imaging being applied.

1. Concealed perception training

In surfing, it has proved valuable to preface ideomotor training with another type of mental imaging: concealed perception training. In this type of mental imaging, the athlete observes himself from an external perspective. In his mind he plays a film of his own wave rides, i.e. he observes the actual wave and imagines himself riding this wave. He replays this several times, with the result that the overall timing of the manoeuvre relative to the interaction of kite and board control, depending on the actual wave, is committed to memory. Once he has done this successfully several times, the athlete can and should switch from the external perspective to the internal perspective. This brings about a change in the primary perception system and leads to the best-proven mental imaging method, ideomotor training.

2. Ideomotor training

For this form of mental imaging it's necessary to visualize the situation in which the action takes place in the present. This is carried out in the framework of the concealed perception training described above. For further successful visualization, it is now imperative to shut out any anxiety that might arise in the real situation, as otherwise this becomes a permanent element of the action.

Now a change of perspective takes place. The surfer no longer sees himself from outside, but from inside. He surfs the wave in his mind and emulates the inner processes that take place when performing the corresponding motions. If executed properly, this even results in the muscles being activated in the way in which they are involved in the target movement, albeit to a lesser extent.[23]

This effect of mental imaging is termed the "Carpenter effect" or also "ideomotor micromovements".[24] In this process, the strength–dynamic component is developed via internal perception[25] by repeated mental self-imaging. During intensive visualization, an increased supply of blood and acceleration of breathing and heart rates have also been shown to occur. This in turn renders it plausible that later when out on the water, the trainee experiences the feeling that he has already been in this situation many times – something that not only makes him more confident in executing the trick, but also prevents the possibility of a blockage due to anxiety.

The crucial criterion for effective

---

23 "When you imagine yourself moving, the muscle groups involved in such an action actually move on a subliminal level" (Syer &Connolly, 1984, p. 48). According to Tiwald (1973, p. 57), mental imaging can also be described as "action with an inhibited final motor link" on account of this fact.
24 Tiwald, 1972, p. 196.
25 Here in particular the kinaesthetic sense and the balancing sense.

mental imaging is the ability to visualize the trick or ride vividly. The figurative perception of a successful trick or a change in an already existing movement image can be underpinned in this case by the photo sequences in Part II. When watching the "internal film" of a trick repeatedly, the athlete should focus his attention specifically on various "key points" of the action.

Carrying out a mental imaging session

If mental imaging is to achieve a successful outcome, the student must be able to imagine his own action as described above from both an external and an internal perspective, and carry this out before and after each training session on the water. In this way, errors in the execution of the manoeuvre can be pinpointed following the session on the water and the "internal film" can be edited. The edited version then needs to be replayed several times in the manner described above prior to the next training unit. The mental imaging itself is undertaken in four stages.

1st stage: The student describes the trick to be practised in his own words in the present, drawing on as many senses as possible.

2nd stage: The student recreates the entire action sequence through self-talk. In this process, it's not yet important for the mental and practical execution to coincide in terms of time; in fact, the entire movement sequence should be observed in the manner of an internal "slow-motion film".[26] This makes it possible to record everything that makes up the action and incorporate it into the "internal film".

3rd stage: The five or six crucial points of the trick as a whole, the so-called "key points" are highlighted, i.e. the elements of the overall action sequence are systematized. For the Aerial, the following key points are conceivable:

1. Following bottom turn, kite back to 11 o'clock or 1 o'clock in the direction of the shore.
2. Approach the lip of the wave.
3. Before reaching the lip, shift the centre of gravity back slightly towards the wave trough.
4. Initiate rotation of the board towards the wave trough while doing so.
5. Let yourself "rebound" off the lip of the wave.
6. Shift weight forward and land.

Thanks to the symbolic marking, the "internal film" is abridged, so that the film takes up a similar length of time to performing the movement in practice.

4th stage: Due to further symbolic marking, these summarized key points can be called up during both the mental and the practical execution of the movement. The following symbols could be used for the Aerial:

1. "Kite 11 o'clock"
2. "Lip"
3. "Weight back"
4. "R-o-t-a-t-e board"
5. "Board straight – **jump**"
6. "F-o-r-w-a-r-d and land"

The degree of expansion or compression of the symbolized key points should help to support the rhythm of the trick and to achieve a correspondence in time between mental and practical execution. If the movement

[26] "However, there are two occasions when you should slow your mental rehearsal down. The first is when you set up the rehearsal program" (Syer & Connolly, 1984, pp. 54–55).

is not carried out at the speed matching the real wave in the visualization, then it will inevitably result in a wipe-out on the water.

It's a good idea to pause a mental imaging session after three to five minutes on one item, to allow time for relaxation between the "films". Performing mental imaging for too long can result in a lapse of the full concentration required for visualization. It is essential that visualization training is concluded with a ride in which everything goes to plan.

Conclusion: Mental imaging cannot take the place of practical training sessions, but it can underpin them. This is because during the learning process, the movement image becomes increasingly differentiated due to the feedback from practical training, and this feedback is then incorporated into the mental picture. This method achieves success more quickly than pure trial and error or correction by another person, since correction doesn't affect one's own image of the actual movement. Carried out properly and in peace, mental imaging offers a superb option for intensifying training processes in kitesurfing the waves and thus optimizing one's ability.

29

Part II: Trainin

Following shore-based preparation, it's now time to go out on the water! This section contains a selection of tips on starting with and riding a wave board through turning and jibe manoeuvres, all the way up to the spectacular barrel ride.

The external conditions must be suited to the training content as much as possible, because the simplest way of learning how to ride a surfstyle board is to start on flat water. This includes starting, riding and jibing or turning the board. The next step consists of getting a feel for being in the wave and riding it without having to steer the kite too much. This is done in onshore conditions with small waves. Only when all the basic principles have been mastered reliably does it make sense to surf in a reef break or a powerful beach break with sideshore conditions. It's advisable to start with small waves here too, to get used to the kite control.

30

Kristin Boese and Sky Solbach.

All the following basics and tricks are demonstrated and described by Kristin Boese, world champion, and Sky Solbach, one of the world's best wave kiters. This will help the reader to assimilate the sequences. In addition, suggestions are given for naming the key points for mental imaging, although as already outlined above, every kiter should formulate the key points in his own words to guarantee effectiveness.

To increase the technical difficulty of the tricks shown for beginners and improvers at a later stage, these can be executed, for example unhooked or without footstraps, i.e. strapless. The possibilities are virtually endless and the variations provide a steady stream of new challenges and successful results, ensuring that the sport lives up to its long prehistory and the mythical aura associated with it.

g on the Water

4 FUNDAMENTALS

31

Starting and riding

Water start

Floating in the water, Kristin leaves her kite in the neutral 12 o'clock position for the time being and places her feet in the subsequent riding position on the board, which she aligns in the riding direction on a beam reach. At the beginning of the start manoeuvre, she steers the kite down slowly in the riding direction and pulls herself onto the board at the same time by flexing her knees sharply. While doing this she begins to apply pressure to the tail of the board with her back leg. Kristin quickly steers the kite deeper into the wind window, generating a strong forward thrust that she utilizes with legs still bent to pull her onto the board. She can now stand up, thereby increasing the pressure her back leg exerts on the board. This stops her from being pulled forwards by the kite, and she can push the board easily onto a downwind course with her front leg, to pick up further speed. Once she has gained speed, she assumes the normal riding position, i.e. she remains with her centre of gravity more over the back third of the board, still has her back leg bent more than the front leg and her upper body opened up slightly in the riding direction.

Compared to starting on a freestyle board, the board here is barely "edged" during the starting manoeuvre. This is due to the fact that the really large fins on the surfstyle board prevent any drift to leeward.

33

Tip:
In light winds it is recommended to fly the kite first back opposite the riding direction and then forwards. This results in the kite flying deeper into the power zone and building up greater pressure, making it easier to pull yourself onto the board when there is little wind.

Key points for mental imaging:
- Kite to 12 o'clock.
- Both legs onto the board and flex knees.
- Steer kite forward and allow self to be pulled onto the board.
- Put pressure on back leg.
- Stand up.

First Kristin aligns her board in the riding direction and stands behind the board on the windward side. The board can be moved into position or held there satisfactorily with the foot, as it will drift slightly to leeward in a strong wind or current. The kite remains in the zenith during this positioning. Now everything happens very quickly. Kristin steers the kite in the riding direction with a short, quick steering movement and simultaneously jumps from the beach with both feet and lands on the board with her feet in the riding position. The distance must be estimated correctly here. When landing on the footpads she still has her body weight evenly distributed on both legs. Now Kristin builds greater power up in the kite by steering it deeper into the wind window. She shifts her weight further over the back leg and pushes her board onto course with the front leg.

34

Key points for mental imaging:

- **Kite to 12 o'clock.**
- **Align board and stand behind it on the wind-ward side.**
- **Steer kite forward and jump onto the board at the same time.**
- **Steer kite further forward and shift weight back.**
- **Bring board onto course.**

Beach start

Riding heelside

When riding straight ahead on your heelside, the surfboard is ridden far flatter than a freestyle board, because in comparison with a freestyle board it is ridden over the fins and not the edge. Here the kite is flown initially in the 11 or 1 o'clock position and the rider's weight is over the rear third of the board. The front leg is almost straight and the back leg is bent. This riding position enables a lot of pressure to be applied to the fins. The upper body opens up towards the riding direction. To be able to maintain the pressure, the kite can be flown deeper in very strong winds provided that one has some experience on a surfboard.

Key points for mental imaging:
- Kite to 11 o'clock or 1 o'clock.
- Shift weight onto back leg.
- Ride board very slightly edged.

When riding toeside too, the rider's weight is over the rear third of the board, i.e. the pressure is transmitted to the board almost entirely via the back leg. To "open up" the body and thus assume a comfortable and functional riding stance, Sky takes his front hand off the bar and places his rear hand in the middle of the bar. The kite is flown in the 11 or 1 o'clock position.

Key points for mental imaging:
- Kite to 11 o'clock or 1 o'clock.
- Weight onto back leg.
- Release front hand and "open up" body.
- Ride board slightly edged.

Riding toeside

TURNING MANOEUVRES

Jibe into switch

Kristin goes upwind slightly before starting the manoeuvre, and during this phase she steers the kite in the new riding direction to create tension in the lines, thereby increasing the dynamics of the turning motion. As soon as the kite flies in the new direction, she takes her rear hand off the bar, transfers her weight forward when changing edge and begins to lay into the carve on a downwind course. In the carve Kristin follows the arc of the kite and maintains the line tension by leaning hard into the carve, thus keeping the jibe radius small. Leaning so heavily into the carve makes it possible for her to drag the inside hand through the water. As well as meriting extra style points, this also supports the movement: by imagining the hand in the water is the pivot point around which she "carves", she can intensify her turning motion. This means that touching the surface of the water supports the turning motion, and this should be done immediately upon changing edges.

Key points for mental imaging:
- Steer kite into the new riding direction and head upwind slightly.
- Steer kite further into the new riding direction and bring weight forward.
- Initiate carve by changing edge.
- Release rear hand.
- Place inside hand on water and lay sharply into the turn.

Jibe from switch

In preparation for this jibe, Sky shifts his weight from the toeside to the heelside. While doing this he steers his kite hard in the new riding direction, thereby increasing the pull on the lines. Then he brings virtually his entire body weight over his heels and leans well into the carve, initially exerting more pressure on the edge via his back leg. By leaning heavily into the carve, he keeps the carve radius small, enabling him to maintain the line tension and adding considerable style to the manoeuvre. While executing the turn – carving – he follows the arc of the kite and brings his weight well forward again.

The critical factor with regard to this jibe, as with nearly all manoeuvres, is the timing. Matching kite control to board control is therefore an essential prerequisite for the success of the trick, as already mentioned above.

The carving jibe can and should be practised as an exercise in kite control for all other tricks too, because poor timing on flat water or in front of waves that are petering out does not pose a hazard. In the bottom turn – in this case riding backside – before waves that are just breaking, or on the wave itself, the consequences of poor timing could be more far-reaching. So it's very important to master the correct timing.

41

Tips:
- If the board is not edged sharply enough, i.e. the turning motion is not aggressive enough, the kite completes the change of direction before the kiter and pulls him "over the edge" of the board.
- If the carve is completed too quickly, the kite loses its tension and eventually pulls the kiter, once he achieves full tension again, over the edge of the board.

Key points for mental imaging:
- Change edge to heelside.
- Steer the kite in the new riding direction.
- Transfer weight to rear heelside and lay into the carve.
- After completing the carve, transfer weight forward again.
- Steer the board straight ahead again.

For the foot change from heelside to toeside, Kristin flies her kite slightly upwards into the 12.30 position and steers her board gently into the wind, to reduce speed. She takes her front hand off the bar, making it easier for her to assume the new position. She can now also use her free arm to adjust her balance in the unsteady rotation movement. Now she makes the foot change by bringing her back foot alongside the front foot in a very short, quick movement to the left and rotating the rear hip in the riding direction. Speedily (almost simultaneously with greater experience) she then shifts her front foot to the rear, concluding the body rotation. Kristin is now in her new riding position.

Tip: Riders who have already gained greater mastery of the surfboard can even "jump round" here. This makes the foot change manoeuvre rather less wobbly, especially on very small boards.

Key points for mental imaging:
• Kite to 11 o'clock or 1 o'clock.
• Release front hand.
• Place back foot next to front foot.
• Rotate and bring front foot to rear.

43

Changing feet into switch

44

Changing

After manoeuvring his kite into the 1 o'clock position, Sky initiates the foot change from toeside to heelside. By turning his hip he introduces the foot changeover, then brings his back foot quickly alongside the front foot. Almost simultaneously he relinquishes the front foot position, brings this foot back and immediately applies pressure to the tail of the board with it. To support and stabilize the stance, he places his front hand on the bar during the foot change and then continues riding normally on the heelside.

45

feet from switch

Key points for mental imaging:
- Kite to 11 o'clock or 1 o'clock.
- Rotate hip and place rear foot next to front foot.
- Place hand back on bar.
- Move front foot backwards.

Tack

Kristin approaches the tack at high speed. If using a board with footstraps, she takes her rear foot out of the strap on the approach to the tack and puts it in front of the strap. Then she begins to steer her kite slowly towards the zenith and in doing so carves powerfully into the wind. To achieve this, she presses very hard with the heel of her back foot on the rear third of the windward edge of her board. At this point in the manoeuvre, good timing dictates success, because she takes advantage of the brief moment during which the kite in the zenith is supporting her weight to jump round. Before jumping, Kristin gives her board a small kick to nudge it into the new riding direction. In the air, she bends her legs, positions them in the new riding direction above the board and lands in the new riding position. Upon landing on the board or just prior to this, Kristin steers the kite in the new riding direction and straightens her board accordingly.

46

Key points for mental imaging:
- Steer kite slowly towards 12 o'clock.
- Place back foot in front of rear strap.
- Apply pressure to rear heelside and cut into the wind.
- Jump round.
- Steer kite forward.

48

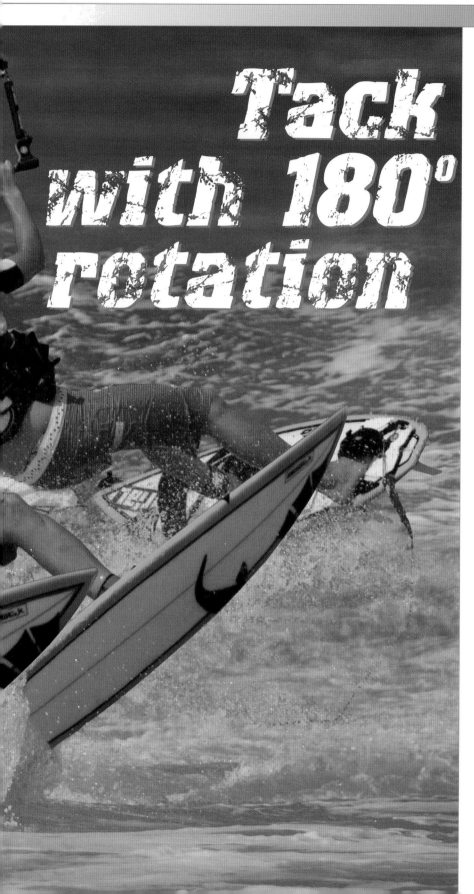

Tack with 180° rotation

For any freestyle kiter who can already perform a backflip transition, this trick should be very easy to learn and can be incorporated satisfactorily as a "stylish" change of direction. Kristin cuts into the wind to start the manoeuvre and steers her kite back in the direction of the wave. At the moment the kite gains sufficient pull upwards, she turns her body and the board through the wind, bending her knees sharply as she does so. She spots her landing and positions the board for a toeside landing while steering the kite into the new riding direction. She lands and rides away on her toeside.

Key points for mental imaging:
- Go to windward.
- Steer kite back in wave.
- Rotate through the wind.
- Spot landing and position board.
- Steer kite forward and continue to ride in switch stance.

49

BASICS FOR KITING IN THE WAVES

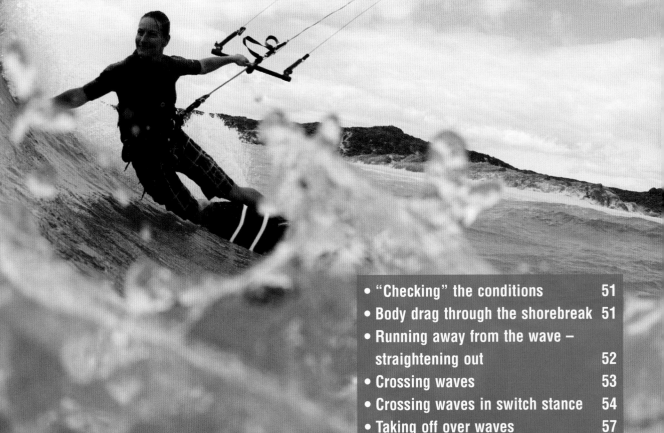

50

"Checking" the conditions

As described above, it's extremely important to check the conditions very carefully before kiting in waves. One should know the general weather situation as well as the tide and how the weather and waves are expected to develop later. The conditions exert a critical influence on the choice of board and kite. In this regard, the wind direction in relation to the waves should be noted in particular, as the technique when crossing the shorebreak in onshore conditions, for example, can be aided by choosing a suitable board and a somewhat bigger kite. A precise knowledge of the subsurface is not only crucial in relation to how the waves break, but should also be noted with reference to any possible hazards at low water and is especially important when entering the water.

51

Body drag through the shorebreak

Kristin observes the waves very carefully.

This type of start is particularly recommended in the case of a shorebreak where it's not possible to place the board on the water and set off using a beach start. It is also useful in an onshore wind, which pushes you towards the beach and makes it difficult to tack for the first few metres.

For the body drag, Kristin lies on her board and holds onto the edge, or a footstrap if there are any. She edges the board, in order to leave the shore zone on a close reach and use her board as a "fin" to counter the wind. She maintains her kite in the 11 o'clock or 1 o'clock position. Going upwind using the body drag is sometimes easier to manage, therefore, than in the riding position and can assist in getting back to the beach in light wind conditions or in emergencies.

Key points for mental imaging:
- Lie on the board and hold on.
- Kite to 11 o'clock or 1 o'clock.
- Edge the windward edge of the board.

Running away from the wave – straightening out

In the beginning it is better to be safe than sorry and in certain situations it is advisable not to attempt riding the wave you are on if you are unsure of what to do. There are situations where you are on your way out and see a big wave coming towards you that may be too big to jump over – in this case it is best to just jibe and ride back towards the shore (chicken jibe). In some cases you may find yourself on a big wave or are too deep in the wave to attempt a turn – in these situations it is better to straighten out, or ride out in front of the wave – just like

Kristin is demonstrating here.

If and when you realize that you are not in the correct position or if the wave is going to close out, simply keep the kite flying forward in the riding direction, keep your speed up and ride straight out

Tip: In some cases the reef can be very shallow in front of the wave which would make straightening out impossible. In these cases it is necessary to kick out through the wave as described later in this chapter.

in front of the wave. In case of a big closing out wave it is important to make sure that you make the decision early enough to avoid having the wave break on top of you.

Key points for mental imaging:
- Observe the wave. If it's too big, make the decision.
- Speed up.
- Keep kite in riding direction and ride out in front of wave.

Crossing waves

When crossing white water, Kristin edges her board hard and approaches the wave on a close reach. To ease the pressure on the board sufficiently to cross the wave, she steers her kite up to the 11 o'clock position. Maintaining her speed, she brings the tip of the board upwards shortly before she reaches the wave. As she crosses the wave, she bends her knees and while still crossing the wave she brings her weight forward again, so as to glide smoothly on.

When crossing waves without footstraps, it is advisable to stand with

Tip: When crossing waves it is important to bring the tip of the board up, as otherwise it will get stuck in the wave.

the back foot a little further forward than when riding straight ahead normally. This ensures that the board runs smoothly and stays well upwind. In addition, this course enables the kiter to keep the speed down, which is important when riding over waves without straps. Before reaching the crest of the wave, the speed is reduced further by edging hard, just as when crossing waves with footstraps, so that the wave can be crossed without taking off. This is aided by bending one's knees sharply, which also makes it easier to stay in contact with the board. After crossing the wave, Kristin straightens her legs again and picks up speed.

Tip: In big waves in particular, it is advisable to steer towards an unbroken part of the wave and cross it here, as large, breaking waves have too much power and speed to be able to cross them while riding. In small waves, however, it is good practice to cross white water and occasionally also negotiate an unbroken section of the wave.

Key points for mental imaging:
- Kite to 11 o'clock or 1 o'clock.
- Go upwind and edge.
- Board tip up.
- Bend knees.
- Cross wave.
- Shift weight forward again.

54

Crossing waves

in switch stance

It is somewhat harder at first to cross waves in the switch stance than on the heelside. However, apart from offering the option of easily being able to change direction quickly, it has the advantage that it is also easy to "carve" onto the wave from this stance, i.e. a change of direction can be undertaken on the wave. As a result, beginners can position themselves in the wave without having to make difficult changes of direction on the wave.

Riding in switch stance across white water is also possible, but here Kristin opts for the better route and heads for the unbroken part of the wave. She goes upwind and takes some of the speed out of the board in this way. To gain a little lift when crossing the wave, she steers the kite back slightly. Shortly before reaching the wave, she moves her centre of gravity backwards, lifting the tip of the board, and bends her knees to cushion the impact on the wave. Immediately after crossing the wave, Kristin steers her kite forward again and continues to ride in switch stance.

55

Key points for mental imaging:
- Go upwind.
- Steer kite back slightly.
- Shift weight backwards.
- Bend knees.
- "Absorb" the wave.
- Steer kite forward again.

56

Riding over waves at high speed almost automatically results in this dynamic mode of crossing waves. Kristin uses a wave that has already broken to take off, but could also achieve this satisfactorily via an unbroken part of the wave. To take off she cuts sharply into the wind. In order to obtain enough lift, Kristin steers her kite back between the 11 o'clock and 12 o'clock position and leans back, which causes the tip of the board to lift. She controls the take-off by bending low with her knees. Directly following take-off, she leans forward again and thus brings the tip of the board back down, stretching her legs again as she does so. In the flight phase she steers her kite forward again in the riding direction. Kristin cushions the landing with her knees.

Tip: If the take-off is executed over the unbroken part of the wave, timing is extremely important: reaching the lip of the wave too late can result in the wave breaking onto the rider, which can have consequences accordingly depending on the wave height!

Taking off over waves

Key points for mental imaging:
- Steer kite back.
- Go upwind.
- Lean back.
- Flex knees.
- Take off.
- Lean forward.
- Steer kite forward.
- Cushion landing.

58

In the situation shown, Sky jumps over a powerful wave that is breaking just in front of him and which he doesn't wish to cross by riding. To do this, he rides at high speed towards the wave, cuts hard upwind and flies his kite back to 12 o'clock, as in a normal jump. He leans back and takes off powerfully. Directly after take-off he pulls the board up under his body by bending his knees. During the flight phase, he brings the tip of the board back down, steers the kite forward and stretches his legs out almost to the full extent again, cushioning the landing with his knees.

In this jump over the breaking wave, one should ensure that the jump is sufficiently high to get over the wave, and that the take-off is executed in sufficient time to leave the water before reaching the wave.

59

Jumping over waves

Key points for mental imaging:
- Steer kite back.
- Go upwind.
- Lean back and take off.
- Pull board up.
- Steer kite forward and bring board tip down.
- Land.

60

However long you spend observing the wave conditions and visualizing them prior to starting, it can always happen that the waves don't run as expected or that your own timing isn't right, and you suddenly find yourself in front of a wave

just about to break and know instantly: "I'm not going to make it." If the wave is breaking on a flat reef, it might be sensible in such a situation not to ride away from it, but to dive through it with the aid of the lift.

Sky edges his board hard and rides directly into the steep, breaking wave. He brings the kite up to the left, so that it pulls him along behind it through the wave. He plunges head and shoulders first forcefully into the wave and pushes the

Kicking out

tip of his board through the wave also, but loses it as he dives through because of the enormously high force of the hollow breaking wave. Sometimes it can also be a good idea to kick the board away before diving through the wave.

Key points for mental imaging:
- Edge hard and head for the wave.
- Steer kite upwards.
- Plunge head and shoulders into the wave.
- "Kick" the board tip through the wave.
- Let yourself be pulled upwards by the kite.

Positioning in the wave

62

When learning to surf, it is easiest simply to ride towards a wave to start with, then to carve onto the wave and on the other edge to kite back towards the shore again. Apart from the edge change from toeside to heelside and vice versa, this is good practice for timing; because in this first step the task may consist of carving your turn gradually into steeper and steeper parts of the wave close to the curl. Practising this will contribute to good timing later when riding nicely "shaped" waves. To do this, the kite is steered into the new riding direction towards the shore just before initiating the carve onto the face of the wave, and then the board is "carved" through the wave slope. Here Kristin rides in switch stance towards the waves and looks for a wave suitable for riding, in order then to "carve onto" it.

Key points for mental imaging:
- Head towards the wave.
- Slowly steer the kite back.
- Start carving on the wave.
- On the other edge continue to kite towards the shore.

2. Once you've mastered carving onto a wave, it's possible to start with advanced positioning on the wave. For this purpose you should observe the waves outside the surf zone (hence further out) and by doing so you'll quickly learn to recognize an incoming set. The bigger the waves, the easier this is. Once you recognize a set, you position yourself "on a wave" and ride with it towards the shore and the "breaking zone".

Sky has already manoeuvred himself into the selected wave here and now tries to position himself as closely as possible to the point at which the wave begins to break on contact with the reef. Since he has observed the wave frequently in mental imaging to gain the external perspective, it's easy for him to find this section on the water. He takes care here not to ride in front of the wave at too great a speed but remains on the wave, to position himself on the upper part of it.

Key points for mental imaging:
- **Find a wave.**
- **Manoeuvre into the wave.**
- **Determine position.**
- **Manoeuvre onto the assumed breaking edge.**
- **Ride in the upper part of the wave.**
- **Wait.**

3. Now the wave begins to break. Kristin has manoeuvred herself to be as close as possible here to the breaking part of the wave and coordinates her timing with the wave. At precisely the moment at which the wave begins to break, she rides down the wave and gets ready for the first bottom turn.

63

Key points for mental imaging:
- **Wait for the right moment.**
- **Ride down the wave.**
- **Start bottom turn.**

Tip: At most spots it's best to pick the second or third wave of a set, as this will have been smoothed by the preceding waves and so there will be fewer wind waves on the swell wave. Another reason is that in the event of a wipe-out, fewer following waves will break directly onto the rider. After the set has gone through, the kiter can then prepare himself for the next set, i.e. get his board back or even relaunch his kite from the water.

5 Surfing basics

We've already pointed out that choosing wind and wave conditions suited to what you want to learn and to your riding ability is very important for success. Before the basics are practised in the different conditions both for regulars and goofies (the following sections are divided accordingly), it's worth bringing to mind once more the advantages and disadvantages of different conditions:

1. **Onshore** conditions: these conditions are best for entering the water, as the kite doesn't have to be steered. It's sufficient just to ride behind the kite, so it can be largely disregarded in the first instance and you can give your full attention to the wave.

2. The appeal of **offshore** conditions lies in the mostly perfect conditions created due to the fact that the wave "breaks clean" and is held up by the wind for a long time. In addition, no wind waves are formed that disrupt the ride. Because the kite doesn't require much steering, it's possible to concentrate entirely on the wave. Nonetheless, riders are advised against kiting in offshore conditions in principle, because even minor mistakes – like losing the board, or simple damage to kit – can have disastrous consequences: self-rescue is impossible in most cases in offshore conditions! We therefore earnestly advise every kiter, even the very experienced, only to go out on the water in such conditions if a rescue boat or jet ski is present and someone is also keeping an eye on the kiter. This is because in an emergency, you will have to battle

against an offshore wind, which is constantly pulling you out of the wave.

For these reasons, we will not look at offshore manoeuvres in the following section. Experienced kiters who nevertheless want to risk this step and are safeguarded by a boat can follow the sideshore manoeuvres, taking care to note that the kite must not be steered so intensively in offshore conditions.

3. Wind from the side – **sideshore**: these conditions are the most demanding yet also the most dynamic, as the kite has to be steered vigorously to keep continuous tension on the lines. In this case, as already mentioned, the timing of the ride must be coordinated with the kite control. Experience suggests that this is what poses the greatest difficulty for beginners.

Depending on the wind–wave configuration, two modes of riding – **frontside** or **backside** – result for kiters according to their preferred stance – **regular** or **goofy**. In frontside riding, the wave kiter stands facing the wave on his board, while in backside riding he has his back to the wave. As we explained in the section "Choice of location",[27] learning the basics is easier with the natural frontside, which means seeking conditions with the wind from the right for regulars and from the left for goofies.

If the opposite conditions prevail, we recommend starting with backside riding. This is not only easier to learn than starting frontside with the "wrong" foot

forward, but is also very attractive with regard to the tricks to be learned: it can be easier to turn vertically straight up the wave face if riding backside and perform extremely dynamic tricks in the breaking section of the lip. In the backside top turn the wave kiter "hangs" over the wave trough and has an unrestricted view downwards, which is highly exhilarating. Apart from this, riders aren't surfing with their natural back foot forward and thus frontside, but backside in their natural stance. And as we have seen, the sport of kitesurfing in the waves has a long history, in which riding techniques have not evolved without reason. This doesn't mean that you shouldn't ride frontside with the "wrong" foot forward at all, because learning tricks on the side other than the natural one has a positive effect on the feeling of movement on the board generally, and equally on the mastery of individual tricks with the natural side forward. In addition, by riding frontside on his non-natural side as well, every kiter can increase his repertoire and continue with the manoeuvres shown in this book in any way he wants. This can be done by practising tricks from the section for the "other foot" (i.e. for goofies, the tricks in the regular section, and vice versa). Each kiter can choose which tricks he wants to learn for himself depending on the conditions, his riding ability and his individual preferences.

---

[27] See section 1.4, p. 16.

Basics for regulars

In any kind of board sports, riders who naturally place their left foot forward are called regular footers. The following section covers moves for regular footers in a variety of conditions.

Onshore wind

With an onshore wind, riding the waves frontside is most natural. However, even in these conditions you have the option to ride in the opposite direction and gain experience of the wave riding backside. On the following pages, some basic manoeuvres are shown for both situations. Since in onshore conditions the wind does not blow 100% onshore in most cases, the tricks vary somewhat, not only in this book but also when practising on the water depending on the wind direction and the angle of the turn, although the sequence remains the same in principle.

66

Pumping up the line

Pumping up the line is a great exercise for every wave-beginner. It enables you to experiment with small waves in onshore conditions and to get a feeling for shifting your weight from rail to rail. You can pump either on your frontside or on your backside, depending on the exact wind direction, which makes it even more versatile.

Kristin is showing a backside variation here which, with an onshore wind coming slightly from the right, is not only good practice for backside riding in bigger waves, but also offers a favourable opportunity to go upwind at the same time – especially when the wind is light, as due to the higher speed on the wave, the apparent wind becomes stronger, amplifying the air flow close to the kite and making it easier to "point high". In addition, pumping on the wave gives the kiter the speed necessary for executing the manoeuvre.

Should the wind come slightly from the

left Kristin would "pump" on her toe side going the other way.

Kristin flies her kite at roughly 45° and has removed her front hand from the bar. She rides close to the wind and generates speed by riding down the wave. This increases the pressure in the kite and enables her to get even closer to the

wind and back to the breaking wave by exerting strong pressure on the heelside. In this way she gets back up the wave face and rides down it anew. The decisive factor in this case is not speed, but the fact that she remains on the wave to take advantage of its power.

Key points for mental imaging:
- **Fly kite at 45°.**
- **Take front hand off the bar.**
- **Go close to the wind.**
- **Ride down the wave.**
- **Get back onto the wave using the heelside.**
- **Ride down the wave again.**

Upwind ride — up the line

68

The wind is blowing side-onshore from the right here and Sky takes the opportunity to ride backside in these onshore conditions. So as to "point" as high as possible while riding up the line, Sky has depowered his kite and applied strong pressure to the heelside, so that no matter how great the power of the wave, he remains on the wave face. He also takes his front hand off the bar. As the wave develops, even top turns are possible, although they are much less spectacular than the ones down the line

to leeward. This way of riding on the "face" of the wave is very good initial practice for the barrel later on.

TIP: In these conditions with side-onshore wind from the right, Sky uses riding on the wave to go upwind at the same time, as due to the higher speed of the wave, the apparent wind becomes stronger and the air flow close to the kite makes it easier to "point high".

Should the wind come from the left here Sky could also go "up the line" on his toeside edge, practising to stay in the wave for later manoeuvres.

Key points for mental imaging:
- Depower the kite.
- Release front hand.
- Apply pressure to heelside.
- Remain as high as possible on the wave face.

69

Bottom turn

A rider always executes a bottom turn when riding into the wave or coming out of a top turn and wanting to get ready for another one, if the wave permits.

Kristin flies her kite in the 1 o'clock position and leans forward into the carve. She applies measured pressure to the toeside of her board. To do this, and to absorb the chop,[28] she flexes her legs sharply. She supports the turning motion by taking her front hand, which is on the inside of the turn, off the bar, as a result of which she can open her upper body towards the wave. Through its contact with the surface of the water, the inside hand also serves as the pivot point around which she executes the carve.

Key points for mental imaging:
- Fly kite to 1 o'clock.
- Release front hand from the bar.
- Open upper body towards the wave.
- Apply pressure to toeside starting from knees.
- Carve.

---

[28] Small wind waves.

Cut back/

The cut back is a top turn, which in contrast to off the lip is not executed precisely into the breaking part of the wave, but in the open face or unbroken part of the wave.

Kristin leaves her kite in the 1 o'clock position in the onshore conditions here, takes her rear hand off the bar and, coming out of the bottom turn, rides towards the wave. On the wave face, she changes edge from toeside to heelside and leans back. As she then carves through the upper part of the wave, she increases the pressure on the heelside further, which adds dynamism to the turn. While carving she keeps an eye on the wave, in order to plan further turns in advance.

re-entry

Key points for mental imaging:
- Fly kite to 1 o'clock.
- Release back hand.
- Weight onto heelside.
- Transfer weight backwards
- Carve.

Off the lip / re-entry

In contrast to the cut back, the off the lip re-entry is not executed in the open face of the wave, but precisely into the breaking and most critical part of the wave.

During the bottom turn, Kristin looks for the wave section into which she intends to carve the off the lip, which determines the ultimate radius of her bottom turn. When changing from toeside to heelside, she shifts her weight right to the back. She carves through the lip of the wave, applying pressure on the heelside. The rear hand, which she has taken off the bar, is now used to maintain her balance. With her front hand she steers the kite if required in the onshore conditions. As soon as Kristin meets the lip of the wave, she shifts her weight forward again and centres it over the board to ride on.

72

Key points for mental imaging:
- **Fly kite to 1 o'clock.**
- **Head for the steepest part of the wave.**
- **Change edge from toe- to heelside.**
- **Shift weight backward.**
- **Carve through the lip of the wave.**
- **Shift weight forward again.**

Sideshore wind from the right – frontside riding

As already described above, starting to ride in conditions with sideshore wind is only recommended once kiting in onshore conditions has been mastered reliably. This is because, in addition to board control when turning and carving on the wave, one has to concentrate here on kite control. For any regular-footer, it will be easiest to begin frontside with the wind from the right in the first instance, as at least this gives the most natural surfing stance.

Kristen rides into the wave or comes out of a top turn here. Well before Kristin starts the bottom turn, she steers the kite back towards the wave to produce a strong pull on the lines, facilitating an extreme turning motion. Then she releases her rear hand from the bar. By turning her upper body towards the wave and leaning at the same time over the toeside towards the centre of the carve, she now initiates the bottom turn at high speed. She supports the subsequent extreme turning motion by dragging the

inside hand through the water; this hand represents an imaginary pivot point around which she carves. Throughout the turn she exerts pressure on the toeside with both feet, but applies greater pressure with the back leg. The carving radius of her turn is geared here to the further development of the wave, which she observes very carefully for this reason. Towards the end of the bottom turn she straightens up again and, in anticipation of the forthcoming top turn, steers the kite back towards the beach.

Key points for mental imaging:
- Steer kite back in the direction of the wave.
- Take rear hand off the bar.
- Exert pressure on toeside.
- Guide inside hand towards centre of turn.
- Carve.

Bottom turn

75

76

Cut back/

Emerging from the bottom turn, Kristin rides towards the wave and steers her kite back towards the shore. After she has ridden up roughly one-third of the wave on the toeside, marking the end of the bottom turn and the start of the cut back, she makes the change from toeside to heelside. As she carves through the upper part and the open face of the wave, she applies roughly 70% of the pressure to the edge via the back leg, until the turn is completed and she is riding down the wave. She keeps an eye on the wave, in order to prepare for further turns.

Key points for mental imaging:
- **Steer kite back towards the shore.**
- **Change to heelside.**
- **Lean backwards.**
- **Carve.**

77

re-entry

Off the lip / re-entry

Emerging from the bottom turn at high speed, Sky steers the kite towards the beach. He changes from toeside to heelside and turns vertically up the face of the wave, directing his attention to the "critical" wave section in which he intends to perform his off the lip. To meet the lip of the wave, he shifts his body weight over his back leg and over onto the heelside. In this way he injects a lot of energy into the top turn, as he counteracts the centrifugal force of the rapid turning motion by edging sharply — carving, thereby producing a large fan of spray. When riding out of the off the lip, he leans well forward again, looks at the wave for further turns and prepares for the next bottom turn.

78

Key points for mental imaging:
- At the end of the bottom turn, steer kite back towards the beach.
- Change to heelside.
- Head for the lip of the wave.
- Lean back and apply strong pressure to heelside.
- Carve.
- At the end of the off the lip, lean forward again.

79

Sideshore wind from the left – backside riding

Backside riding in sideshore conditions initially poses a major challenge. Experience indicates that familiarizing yourself with the unaccustomed movement sequences in backside riding to the point where they can be executed automatically takes a little longer than in frontside riding. Wave kiters are often in the situation, however, where they encounter other, changing conditions in different spots. To be able to have fun in all situations, it is therefore seriously recommended that kiters learn backside riding, and they will be rewarded with exciting, spectacular rides.

Bottom turn

Coming out of a top turn or just riding into the wave, Kristin steers her kite in the direction of the wave and starts the turning motion by exerting a lot of pressure on the heelside using her back leg. She rotates her upper body towards the carve as she does this. She gears the carving radius to the wave and thus also the pressure she applies, as she is looking to hit a certain section of the wave for the forthcoming top turn. The transfer of weight and high speed result in a highly dynamic turning motion.

Key points for mental imaging:
- Steer kite back towards the wave.
- Transfer weight to back leg.
- Apply strong pressure to heelside.
- Bend knees.
- Carve.

Cut back/

While still at the end of the bottom turn, Sky steers the kite towards the shore, thereby generating strong tension on the lines. He takes his rear hand off the bar and while riding vertically up the wave face he switches from heelside to toeside. For the top turn on the toeside at the top of the wave, he brings his weight over his back leg and carves around the imaginary pivot point created by his hand in the water. This adds dynamism to the carve and throws spray. When riding down the open face of the wave he centres himself briefly over the board so that, after switching back to heelside once again, he can get ready for the next bottom turn. He observes the wave very carefully here, so that he can adapt the radius of his next turn to it.

82

Key points for mental imaging:
- **Steer kite back.**
- **Release rear hand.**
- **Shift weight to toeside and backwards.**
- **Carve.**
- **Transfer weight forward again and change to heelside.**

re-entry

84

Off the lip/ re-entry

Since the most critical section of the wave has to be met exactly, this manoeuvre calls for extremely good timing, for which extensive experience is required.

After Sky has completed the bottom turn, he steers his board almost vertically up the wave towards the lip. While doing this, he steers his kite back towards the beach and takes his rear hand off the bar. At the moment of contact with the lip, he supports the turn by turning his head and upper body clearly towards the wave trough. Here he literally rebounds off the white water, bending his knees well to absorb the pressure. Sky drags his inside hand through the water and carves around his hand as an imaginary pivot point. After completing the top turn, he uses his free arm to help maintain his balance, leans forward again and rides down the wave to get ready for the next bottom turn.

85

Key points for mental imaging:
- Steer board towards lip.
- Steer kite back in direction of beach.
- Take rear hand off the bar.
- Rotate head and upper body towards wave trough.
- Push board round with back leg.
- Transfer weight forward.
- Ride down the wave.

Basics for goofies

Kiters who ride naturally with their right foot forward in the wave are called *goofies*. This stance is by no means a disadvantage! Most well-known, good wave kiting spots are even noted goofy spots. In this section we show the wave basics for *goofies*.

Onshore wind

With an onshore wind, frontside riding is easiest to begin with, because it's on the more natural side. But because the wind is blowing onshore more or less at a right angle, this also affords an opportunity for you to try your first efforts at backside riding and prepare for a wide variety of manoeuvres. Depending on the angle of the wind and your own preference, the program can be varied considerably and the trick options are virtually unlimited. In addition, when practising in onshore conditions, the major advantage lies in the fact that no great risk is incurred for the reasons already discussed. You need to take care not to "ride underneath" the kite, though, in all onshore turns.

Upwind Ride

This riding "up the line" is a great opportunity to get used to kiting in the waves. You are in the wave, exploring its power, speed and form but are not doing any critical manoeuvres yet. Riding up the line is possible on your toeside or on your heelside, depending on the exact direction of the onshore wind. Sky is showing us the backside version in side-onshore winds from the left.

So as to "point" as high as possible, Sky has depowered his kite and applied strong pressure to his heelside. Thus no matter how powerful the wave, he remains on the wave face. He takes his front hand off

Tip: In this situation with side-onshore conditions from the left, Sky uses riding on the wave to go upwind at the same time, as due to the higher speed on the wave, the apparent wind becomes stronger and the air flow close to the kite makes it easier to "point high".

the bar. Even top turns are possible going upwind, although less spectacular than those to leeward due to the lower speed. This is also good preliminary practice for barrel rides later on.

Key points for mental imaging:
- Depower the kite.
- Release front hand.
- Apply pressure to heelside.
- Remain as high as possible on the wave face.

87

Pumping up the line is a great way to get used to riding waves and feeling the power they generate without having to steer the kite. Shifting your weight from rail to rail, you can pump up the line and learn to generate speed for manoeuvres later on. As Kristin drops down the wave face, she flies her kite at roughly 45 degrees and removes her front hand from the bar. She now shifts her weight onto her heelside and pumps back up the wave face and then repeats this action. This not only helps her get a feeling for wave riding but also helps her go upwind due to the speed of the wave and the apparent wind it generates in her kite. This backside manoeuvre is a good basis for practising later backside manoeuvres in sideshore winds.

88

Pumping up

Key points for mental imaging:
- Fly kite at 45°.
- Take front hand off the bar.
- Go close to the wind.
- Ride down the wave.
- Get back onto the wave by putting pressure on the heelside.
- Ride down the wave again.

the line

89

90

Bottom turn

91

Kristin flies her kite in the 11 o'clock position and leans forward into the carve. She applies measured pressure to the toeside of her board, putting rather greater pressure on the back leg. To absorb the chop,[29] she bends her legs

sharply. She aids the turning motion by turning her upper body towards the wave and taking her front hand on the inside of the carve off the bar, so as to bring it towards the surface of the water. Touching the surface thus acts as an imaginary pivot point around which to execute the carve.

[29] Small wind waves.

Key points for mental imaging:
- Fly kite to 11 o'clock position.
- Release front hand from the bar.
- Exert pressure on the toeside starting from the knees.
- Rotate upper body towards the wave.
- Carve.

For this top turn in the open face or non-breaking part of the wave, Kristin leaves her kite in the 11 o'clock position, takes her rear hand off the bar and rides towards the wave as she comes out of the bottom turn. On the wave face, she makes the edge change from toeside to heelside and brings her weight back. As she subsequently carves through the upper part of the wave, she increases the pressure on the heelside, adding a dynamic element to the turn. Throughout the turn she watches very carefully as the wave develops, so as to plan further turns in advance.

Key points for mental imaging:
- **Kite to 11 o'clock.**
- **Release rear hand.**
- **Change to heelside.**
- **Transfer weight back.**
- **Carve.**

92

Cut back/ re-entry

Once again, near-perfect timing is crucial in the off the lip, the top turn into the breaking lip, as the moment in which the wave starts to break is extremely short.

Kristin flies the kite to the 11 o'clock position or leaves it there, and during the bottom turn she seeks out the wave section into which she intends to carve the off the lip, which determines the final radius of her bottom turn. When changing from toeside to heelside she brings her weight right back. Having taken her rear hand off the bar, she uses it now to maintain her balance. To the extent that it is necessary in onshore conditions, she steers the kite with her front hand, always taking care to keep sufficient tension in the lines. As soon as Kristin reaches the lip of the wave, she transfers her weight forward again and centres it over the board to ride away.

94

Key points for mental imaging:
- Fly kite to 11 o'clock.
- Head for the steepest part of the wave.
- Change edge from toe- to heelside.
- Transfer weight backwards.
- Carve through the lip of the wave.
- Transfer weight forward again.

Off the lip

/re-entry

Sideshore wind from the left — frontside riding

Frontside riding is a natural, beautiful way of surfing waves. If this is mastered in onshore conditions, it can be practised in sideshore conditions. In time, bigger waves can also be selected. An important factor for riding with the wind from the side, as described above, is the timing of the kite control. This should be learned first without turns, then with turns, and committed to memory.

96

Bottom turn

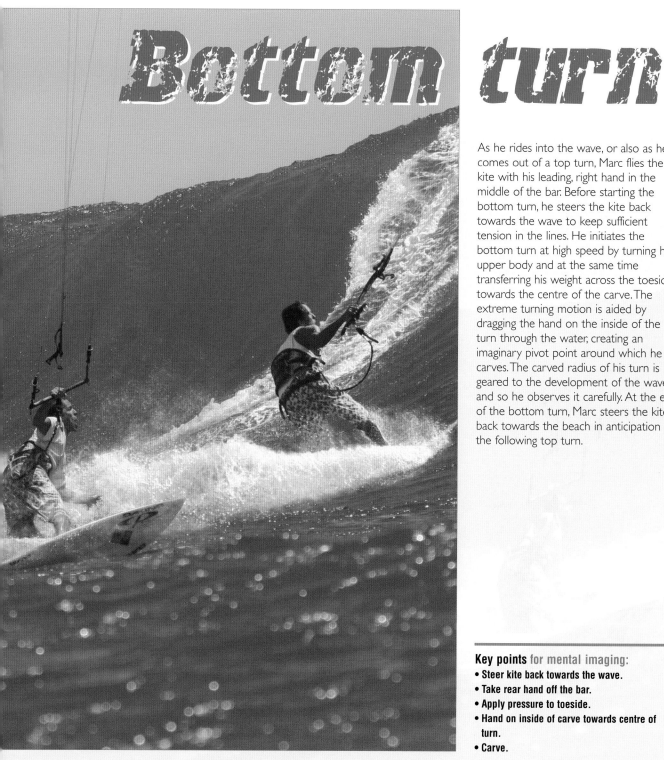

As he rides into the wave, or also as he comes out of a top turn, Marc flies the kite with his leading, right hand in the middle of the bar. Before starting the bottom turn, he steers the kite back towards the wave to keep sufficient tension in the lines. He initiates the bottom turn at high speed by turning his upper body and at the same time transferring his weight across the toeside towards the centre of the carve. The extreme turning motion is aided by dragging the hand on the inside of the turn through the water, creating an imaginary pivot point around which he carves. The carved radius of his turn is geared to the development of the wave, and so he observes it carefully. At the end of the bottom turn, Marc steers the kite back towards the beach in anticipation of the following top turn.

97

Key points for mental imaging:
- Steer kite back towards the wave.
- Take rear hand off the bar.
- Apply pressure to toeside.
- Hand on inside of carve towards centre of turn.
- Carve.

98

Cut back/

99

re-entry

In contrast to an off the lip, the cut back, or re-entry, is not executed precisely into the breaking part of the wave, but into the unbroken part (or open face) of the wave.

Kristin comes out of the bottom turn and rides up the wave. She steers her kite back towards the shore and, while still on the lower part of the wave, switches from toeside to heelside. As she carves through the upper part of the wave, she leans back, so that she transmits roughly 70% of the pressure to the edge via her back leg. She watches the wave carefully to leeward, to plan further turns.

Key points for mental imaging:
- Steer kite back towards the shore.
- Change to heelside.
- Transfer weight backwards.
- Carve.

Kristin comes out of the bottom turn at high speed, watches the wave develop very carefully and steers the kite towards the beach. She switches from toeside to heelside and rides up the face of the wave. She focuses her attention on the ''critical'' wave section into which she intends to carve the off the lip. Shortly before she meets the lip of the wave, she shifts her body weight back over her back leg and over onto the heelside. This adds high dynamics to her turning motion and she throws lots of spray. At the end of the off the lip, she transfers her weight forward again, watches the wave for further turns and approaches the next bottom turn.

100

Key points for mental imaging:
- At the end of the bottom turn, steer the kite back towards the beach.
- Change to heelside.
- Head for the lip of the wave.
- Transfer weight backwards and apply strong pressure to heelside.
- Carve.
- At the end of the top turn, transfer weight forward again.

Off the lip

/re-entry

Sideshore wind from the right – backside riding

Backside riding will feel very unfamiliar to start with and it will take a little time to develop a comfortable, secure feeling, but this will then be rewarded with thrilling rides. Initial experience of backside riding should be gained in onshore conditions; the kiter can then practise with sideshore wind.

102

Bottom turn

103

Coming out of a top turn, or after dropping into the wave, Kristin steers her kite back in the direction of the wave. She applies considerable pressure to the heelside via her back leg, initiating the turning motion. She supports the turn by rotating her upper body in the carve direction too. As she aims to meet the section for the top turn coming up, she adjusts the edge pressure and thus the carve radius to the wave or the probable development of the wave.

Key points for mental imaging:
- Steer kite back towards the wave.
- Shift weight onto back leg.
- Apply strong pressure to heelside.
- Bend knees.
- Carve.

104

Cut back/

Towards the end of the bottom turn, Sky steers the kite towards the shore, thereby increasing the tension on the lines. Following this steering movement, he releases his rear hand from the bar and changes from heelside to toeside as he rides up the wave face. For the re-entry on the upper part of the wave, he shifts his weight over his back leg and carves around the imaginary pivot formed by his hand in the water. When riding down the unbroken part of the wave (open face), he centres himself over the board again. Following a further edge change back to heelside, he can prepare for the next bottom turn. He observes the further development of the wave, in order to adapt his next manoeuvres accordingly.

105

Key points for mental imaging:
- **Steer kite back towards shore.**
- **Release rear hand.**
- **Transfer weight to toeside and backward.**
- **Carve.**
- **Shift weight forward again and centre it over the board.**

re-entry

106

This manoeuvre calls for very good timing, as the lip of the wave must be met exactly.

After completing the bottom turn, Sky steers his board as steeply as possible up the wave towards the lip. He steers his kite back towards the beach and takes his rear hand off the bar. At the moment of contact with the lip, he turns his head and his upper body in the direction of the wave trough and pushes the board round powerfully with his back foot. He bends his knees, to absorb the impact of contact with the wave, literally rebounds off the lip of the wave and drags the hand on the inside of the turn through the water, executing the turn around his hand as an imaginary pivot. After completing the off

Off the lip/ re-entry

the lip, he uses his free arm to help maintain his balance, brings his weight forward again, rides down the wave and prepares for the next bottom turn.

Key points for mental imaging:
- Steer board towards the lip.
- Steer kite back towards beach.
- Take rear hand from bar.
- Turn head and upper body towards wave trough.
- Push board round using back leg.
- Transfer weight forward.
- Ride down the wave.

6 Wave manoeuvres and tricks for advanced kiters

108

The list of wave manoeuvres to try out and learn is virtually endless. Unhooked, strapless, with board flips and rotations – basic riding can be expanded by any manner of means. Below we offer just a small selection of the key manoeuvres for advanced kiters. We don't want to impose limits on your imagination though.

Tack with body 180

Kristin approaches the manoeuvre by going hard upwind and steering the kite back to almost 12 o'clock at the same time. She carves the board through the wind as far as possible and follows this with her entire body into the turning motion. At the moment at which she can ride no further through the wind, she lets herself be pulled upwards by the kite and quickly switches the position of her feet, putting her back foot before the front

one and moving the front foot back. When doing this you need to keep a close eye on the board and focus on the new foot position. As soon as this new position has been assumed, the weight must be distributed uniformly to both feet again. Kristin supports this by steering her kite forward into the new riding direction with what is now her front hand, to generate sufficient power to ride on.

Key points for mental imaging:
- **Go upwind.**
- **Kite to 12 o'clock.**
- **Carve through the wind, turn body while doing this.**
- **Place back foot ahead of front foot.**
- **Bring front foot back.**
- **Steer kite forward into the new riding direction.**

110

Backroll

For this trick Sky looks for a small wave that has petered out or a small wind wave and cuts sharply upwind at the right moment. He pulls the kite back slowly towards 12 o'clock. If the kite steering is properly coordinated with reaching the wave – as can be seen here – the wave "kicks" him out of the water. On take-off, Sky starts rotating from the middle of his body. As he does so, he controls the board with his feet and edges it so that the wind presses it onto his feet. This gives him enough time to grab the rail of his board as far forward as possible. Once holding firmly onto his board, he turns it into the new direction, bringing the 180° body rotation to an end. Then he brings the board back into the correct position and the new riding direction under his feet, releases his grip from the rail and concentrates on landing. At the moment he lands, he steers his kite quickly forward to gain enough power for riding on.

111

Key points for mental imaging:
• Head for a small wave.
• Go upwind and steer kite slowly to 12 o'clock.
• Take off, edge board and start rotating.
• Grab rail.
• Turn board in the new direction.
• Release hand from rail and land.

transition strapless

112

Sky rides at high speed towards a small "ramp", keeping the kite at 45°. He then cuts upwind sharply to generate lots of energy for the take-off and steers the kite back. As he takes off, he brings his weight forward so that he is as upright as possible, and takes his rear hand off the bar. The decisive factor is that he angles his board in the air so that it is pressed onto his feet by the wind. At the highest point of the jump he "depowers" his kite a little and thus initiates the landing. He

centres his weight over the board and steers the kite forward again. Sky cushions the landing with his knees and rides on.

Key points for mental imaging:
- Hold kite at 45°.
- Seek out a small "ramp".
- Go upwind and steer kite back.
- On take-off, bring weight forward and take rear hand off the bar.

- Angle the board.
- Depower the kite.
- Centre weight over the board.
- Steer kite forward and land.

114

Tail slide

The tail slide can be executed both in the unbroken part of the wave and in the breaking wave section. Here Sky performs it in onshore conditions in the steep part of a relatively small wave, which has proved extremely useful in learning this difficult manoeuvre.

At the moment at which Sky comes out of the bottom turn, he steers the kite hard forward using his front hand. He uses his free rear arm to help keep his balance. As he changes edge from toeside to heelside, he begins to carve the board strongly by way of his back leg. He does this so hard and for so long that the fins eventually break loose and the tail lifts out. At just this moment, Sky transfers his weight forward again. With his rear hand and a counter-rotation of his upper body, Sky prevents his board from continuing to rotate in a full 360, and regains the normal riding position.

115

Key points for mental imaging:
- Steer kite to 1 or 11 o'clock.
- Steer kite hard forward.
- Shift weight onto back leg.
- Carve with maximum force.
- When the tail lifts out, transfer weight forward again.
- Counteract further rotation of the board using the hand and by counter-rotating the upper body.

116

Kristin rides out of the bottom turn with her upper body facing the wave and travels at maximum speed towards the wave section that she has chosen for the aerial. She flies the kite here in the 1 o'clock position and has taken the back hand off the bar. She must keep a careful eye on the section, as she must watch for the exact moment at which the wave breaks to take off. Shortly before contact with the lip, she executes a swift edge change from toeside to heelside. In the brief moment of contact with the lip, she moves her weight forward and upward, so that she can utilize the wave's energy for take-off or more for a kind of rebound from the lip. During flight she remains centred over the board with her weight forward and can even grab the rail of the board while doing so, in order to land upright.

Frontside aerial

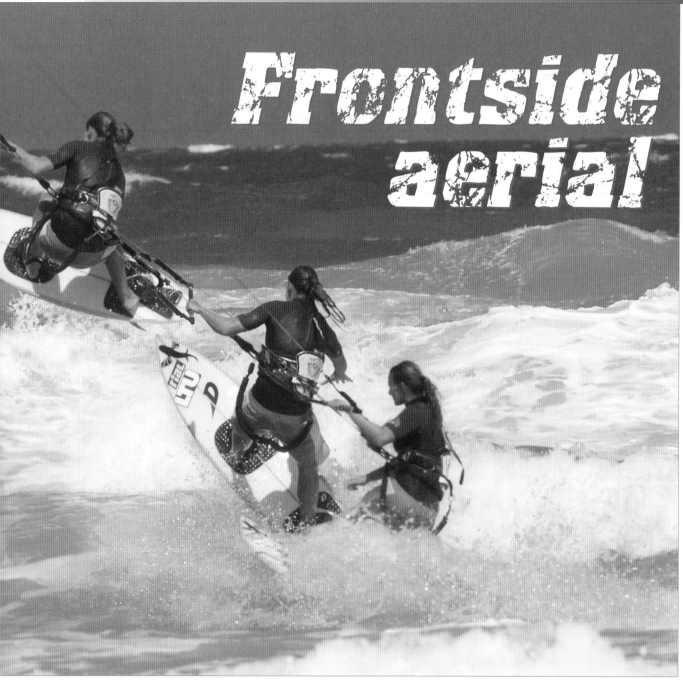

117

The key to the success of this trick lies in hitting the right section of the wave at the right moment, so that the wave takes on the job of catapulting you out of the water.

Key points for mental imaging:
- Steer kite to 11 o'clock.
- Seek out take-off point and ride towards this in switch stance.
- Change to heelside.
- Shift weight forward and upwards.
- Allow yourself to be catapulted out by the wave.
- Centre weight above board.
- Land.

Backside aerial

Sky flies his kite to the 11 o'clock position, takes his rear hand off the bar and carves a backside bottom turn towards the wave. He focuses on the breaking part of the wave so as to meet it precisely for take-off. To do this, he begins the top turn a little later than he normally would when doing an off the lip and pushes his board around hard using his back foot. Because Sky meets the section precisely as it is breaking, it projects him up and out of the wave. Before landing he centres his weight over the board once more.

Key points for mental imaging:

- Fly kite to 11 o'clock.
- Take rear hand off the bar.
- Carve heelside towards the wave.
- Press board into the lip of the wave with the back foot.
- Lift off.
- Centre weight.
- Land.

The floater is an extremely stylish and functional trick, which enables the kiter to cross over a fast-breaking section of the wave without having to bottom turn around it.

Kristin emerges from the bottom turn at high speed and steers the kite towards the shore in anticipation of the floater. She doesn't ride vertically up the face of the wave, but instead manoeuvres at a considerably flatter angle to the breaking section.

She directs the nose of her board towards the back of the wave and climbs on top of the breaking section. She then glides across the top of the breaking section, centring her weight over the board. To end the floater, she transfers her weight forward and onto the heel side to drop back into the trough of the wave. She keeps herself centred and

balanced over the board so as to stick the landing and get ready for the next bottom turn.

Key points for mental imaging:
- Ride at high speed towards the lip of the wave.
- Steer kite back towards the shore.
- When you reach the lip, point board towards the back of the wave.
- Centre weight over board.
- Float.
- Transfer weight forward and follow the kite.
- "Drop" down the breaking wave, centring your weight as you do so.

Floater

121

Unhooked frontside bottom and top turn

123

For this manoeuvre, Sky rides at high speed into the wave and unhooks. At the same time, he edges his board hard and thereby produces a strong pull on the lines. When he gets to the bottom of the wave, he steers the kite aggressively back towards the wave. At the beginning of the bottom turn, he takes his rear hand off the bar and places his front hand in the middle. This helps Sky to pull the kite down with the front hand which keeps tension on the lines throughout the turn. When carving through the bottom turn, he applies pressure to virtually the entire

toeside, which he achieves by leaning forward, bringing his rear hand to the surface of the water at the centre of the carve and absorbing the pressure with his knees. As soon as Sky begins to ride up the wave, he steers the kite towards the shore with his front hand. At the top of the wave he shifts his weight to the heelside and *carves* the *turn* into the wave face. Depending on the nature of the subsequent top turn and the forces generated, the following turn can be performed either with just the front hand on the bar or with both hands.

Key points for mental imaging:
- **Ride into the wave at speed and unhook.**
- **Steer kite back towards the wave.**
- **Place front hand in the centre of the bar and release rear hand.**
- **Change from heelside to toeside.**
- **Carve through the bottom turn.**
- **Steer kite back towards the shore.**
- **Begin top turn.**

124

Frontside 360

For this trick, Sky rides unhooked into the bottom turn. As in a backside aerial he rides out of the bottom turn with his back to the wave and rides at maximum speed towards a steep, breaking wave section. He steers the kite towards the shore again as he does this. Due to the fact that he meets the wave right at its lip, he is practically "catapulted out" by the wave's force. Just as he lifts off, he takes his back hand off the bar and starts rotating from the middle of his body

about his own axis, supporting this motion by turning his head also. During the manoeuvre he keeps his knees bent and draws his body up as much as possible throughout the rotation. Then he reaches around his back for the bar with his back hand, passes the bar and rotates his body 360°. To end the rotation, he quickly stretches out again and lands with his knees bent.

Key points for mental imaging:
- **Steer kite towards the shore.**
- **Look out for a take-off point and ride towards it.**
- **Allow yourself to be catapulted out by the wave.**
- **Take back hand off the bar and rotate.**
- **Bend knees and draw body up.**
- **Reach around your back for the bar with your back hand.**
- **Pass bar.**
- **Land.**

Riding in the barrel is the ultimate kick for all kitesurfers and surfers. In this manoeuvre, the surfer is briefly engulfed in the breaking wave, which is an unforgettable experience. If the ride in the wave has been timed properly, the surfer comes surfing out of the "green room" at the end of the rolling wave again at high speed.

Since good timing is crucial for the success of "getting barrelled", during his ride on the mounting wave Marc monitors closely how it builds up and begins to break. To ensure a successful ride into the wave, he looks for a very steep part of the wave that is breaking into shallow water. While doing this he takes a high line on the wave face. To stay close to the steepest part of the wave, he takes his rear hand off the bar and applies extremely strong pressure to the toeside of his board while leaning towards the breaking part of the wave. However corrections may be necessary to trim his position on the wave. Now the wave begins to break over him. If necessary he squats down on his board. He continues to ride toeside in the tube and heads for the exit from the barrel. Having emerged from the wave, he rides towards the channel and away from the breaking wave.

Key points for mental imaging:
- **Fly kite to 1 o'clock.**
- **Remain on the upper part of the wave.**
- **Apply strong pressure to toeside and carve towards the steepest part of the wave.**
- **Remain close to the wave and let it "engulf" you.**
- **Bear away as you emerge from the wave.**
- **Ride out of the wave and into the channel.**

Barrel going downwind

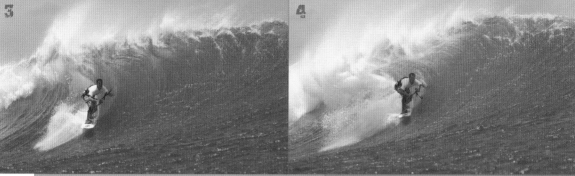

Part III: Additional training activities

When it comes to learning or improving tricks and to the specific physical factors involved, the best practice for kitesurfing in the waves is – undoubtedly – kitesurfing in the waves. But the days in the year on which the waves break perfectly and the wind is both of a suitable strength and is blowing from the right direction are unfortunately few and far between. And even then we still have to be in the right spot. This poses the question of whether options exist for getting practice without having to head out onto the water, so that when the day with perfect conditions dawns, you'll be well prepared to take to the ocean. The straight answer to this question is "yes". There are wide-ranging possibilities and activities that are highly beneficial, provided that they are undertaken regularly and with the necessary concentration and reflection. As well as the mental imaging described above, there are various other forms of training that directly underline kitesurfing skills or improve the basis for these.

126

7 Crossover: related sports disciplines

As we stated at the beginning, seen from a historical perspective, **surfing** is the mother of kitesurfing in the waves. When looking at these two relations, however, we realise that surfing could very well be its sister, and perhaps even its little sister in waves that aren't so spectacular. We shall not explore this aspect further here, but it is obvious that the forerunner of all forms of surfing, namely wave riding, offers the best option as a training activity, both for

kitesurfing practice and for having lots of fun. If a sports discipline such as this helps you to learn another sport, then a transfer effect occurs that is termed crossover. This applies perfectly to surfing when we think about learning how to kitesurf in the waves. Many of the world's best wave kiters come from a surfing background. Their surfing ability is therefore an aid to learning another type of sport. This type of learning transfer is called proactive transfer. The advice to wave kiters to take up surfing as an additional sport is based on a so-called retroactive transfer: in this case, learning the new sports discipline can improve their ability in the sport they already engage in if the two have common features. In addition to the fun factor that surfing also offers, this recommendation is backed up by the fact that there are many days on which there is no wind, but good waves. And it would be an awful pity not to take advantage of these!

There are several other sports that can positively assist with kitesurfing in the waves. The decisive criterion in choosing a complementary sport, provided that the opportunities for engaging in it are comparable, should be its similarity with regard to the profile of requirements. This relates on the one hand to the external conditions, but also to the nature of the actions performed in particular, and how these are controlled. It is not sufficient, for example, just to take the medium of water as a criterion for the possibility of learning transfer. For instance, although sailing is performed on the water, it is far

removed from kitesurfing in the waves with regard to the actions involved – unlike snowboarding, which obviously takes place in a completely different environment, but is related to kitesurfing in terms of movement. This training option is illustrated briefly below with reference to three sports that are beneficial for the transfer process:

Wakesurfing: In this offshoot of wakeboarding and kitesurfing in the waves, the surfer gets into the boat's wake on his board with the aid of the rope. As it develops, this wave then gives him the power for his "surf ride". The kite can be imitated very successfully by the pull of the rope. Letting go of the rope makes it possible to get a feel for the power of the wave.

Sea kayaking: Apart from being good fun for all water sports enthusiasts, sea kayaking offers beginners in particular a great opportunity to gain their first experience of waves, especially with regard to the power that a wave

Kristin out wakesurfing.

127

Frontside bottom turn on the "frozen wave".

generates. This experience can then be drawn on when kiting in waves.

Skateboarding: Because it can easily be practised at any time, this sport is especially suitable for helping you to learn kitesurfing in the waves. Anyone with good skateboarding skills and sufficient opportunity – along with the necessary protective equipment – can prepare themselves for manoeuvres on the wave by practising weight transfer in the half-pipe and applying pressure to the edge and rollers at the top edge of the half-pipe in the backside turn and frontside turn. This is only recommended for skateboard wizards, however, because the risk of injury – even with protective equipment – should be regarded as very high!

⑧ Physiological prerequisites for training

The stresses that occur in kitesurfing in the waves are manifold. On the one hand, it is very demanding physically, while on another level the need to make rapid decisions on how to respond to the constantly changing conditions must be taken into account. This means that the changing effects of forces acting on the body during manoeuvres must be quickly recognized and the planned sequence of movements tailored to these. This applies to even the smallest positional changes, which are detected by the proprioceptive system consisting of neuromuscular and tendon spindles and the joint receptors. A stabilizing reaction follows automatically. The ability to protect yourself against injury, which is improved by suitable training, is of considerable significance here: it has been shown that kitesurfers who have had extensive neuromuscular training in particular suffer fewer injuries than those who have not. If avoiding injuries is not sufficient argument for the need to adopt a suitable fitness regime, then the following surely is: with a good level of fitness not only can you spend longer out on the water, but your performance will also be much better. This is because an athlete with good neuromuscular training can react significantly faster to compensate for changes in his situation.

How therefore should you prepare for the stresses that occur in kitesurfing in the waves?

Power

Compared to freestyle, the power component plays a less important role in kitesurfing in the waves. This is largely due to the fact that the kite fulfils a different function in this discipline, namely that of generating sufficient propulsion for gliding. A wave kiter doesn't need the power that a freestyle kiter requires to obtain the necessary lift for his tricks. The comparatively bigger board in relation to freestyle emphasizes this point and makes it possible to select a smaller kite.

Nonetheless, just as in freestyle kiting, performance is also improved in kitesurfing in the waves if the potential power is suitable. The level of interaction of potential power components is crucial here: depending on the speed, the force to be applied for steering the board is sometimes extremely high. The steering momentum comes from the middle of the body and is transmitted to the board via the legs. It is supported by rotating the head and upper body. Against this background, you are advised not to engage in weight training of isolated muscle groups, as many people do in the gym, but rather in work-outs aimed at overall, integrated muscle strengthening. It is especially desirable in this regard to include the balancing function, because power is always deployed out on the water according to the prevailing state of equilibrium. As in other sports, each intended movement, or even a movement that is in the process of being executed, is reviewed to see if it can be reconciled with keeping your balance. This means in turn that you must be aware of your constantly changing state of balance. This awareness needs to be developed too, as the strength developed in this way will be "intelligent" and thus take account of the profile of requirements for situation-dependent sports. You should pay attention to this in particular if the sport

Rear leg lift: This exercise for strengthening the core muscles is performed with your eyes closed.

for which you are training is subject to external factors that influence your balance as well as to changes in your physical position. Another factor to be considered in kitesurfing in the waves is that the power of the wave deflects the direction of gravity. These conditions, which influence one another in a variety of ways, should be taken into account as far as possible in a weight training routine tailored to the respective sport.

As already mentioned above, the movements used in kitesurfing originate in the centre of the body. This means that this core should be strengthened. By way of example, two exercises are shown to achieve this, taking balance into account:

1. "Rear leg lift" with eyes closed: Closing your eyes has the effect of preventing you from relying automatically on your sense of sight for adjusting your balance. This makes it possible to rely solely on the sense of balance, which always works in conjunction with the kinaesthetic or so-called "muscle sense", when adjusting the amount of power applied. In this exercise it is important to move slowly from the starting position into the balance, hold this position for approximately 2 seconds and then slowly return to the starting position, but without putting your foot down completely, in order then to move from this position back into the balance etc. You should perform the exercise with concentration until you can no longer keep your balance, which is a clear sign of fatigue.

This core exercise also strengthens the hips.

2. Strengthening the core and hips: This exercise should also be performed with your eyes closed, to develop the interaction between power and sense of balance. The body should form a straight line from head to foot in this exercise also. Raise one arm and the opposite leg, hold for two seconds and then swap arm and leg over. This exercise can be performed until you feel a clear sense of fatigue that makes it very difficult or even impossible to maintain your balance.

131

3. Jumping around from a low step position: In this exercise, Kristin takes care not to touch the ground with her back leg. After going down into the squat on one side, she springs up quickly enough to be able to switch legs while briefly in the air and land in a low squat on the other side. She performs the exercise again, but with the other leg forward this time. To make this exercise harder, you can hold dumb-bells while performing it.

Further exercises, which should be performed according to the same principle, can be found in the Bibliography at the back of the book.

You can introduce a "power" element to this exercise by using dumb-bells.

Neuromuscular training

Various studies of athletes who are subject to constant and sometimes unpredictable changes in situation have shown that ongoing neuromuscular training can significantly reduce the number of injuries suffered. This is due to the fact that the exercises unite conditioning and coordinative abilities.[30] The proprioception of the muscles, joints and tendons can be improved in this way, which not only reduces the risk of injury when kitesurfing but also improves sensitivity to your own movements and thus performance. The neuronal connections are strengthened and a rapid, automatic response to sudden changes of situation becomes possible.

The proprioceptive and neuromuscular element of the two strengthening exercises described above is increased by carrying them out with your eyes closed. There are a large number of exercises in this form that can be incorporated into daily life without taking up too much time:

1. Balancing on the "wobble board" or another unsteady base, first on both feet, then on one foot, with eyes closed. These exercises strengthen the ankle joint muscles in particular and improve proprioception in this area.

2. Jumps from a small elevation onto a soft floor mat or the sand, first with eyes open and then with them closed. This exercise strengthens the entire leg as well as the ankle joint muscles and stabilizes the knee joint by improving neuromuscular perception.

3. Multiple opportunities exist for neuromuscular training in everyday situations and these can be spotted everywhere once the principle has been understood. One particularly interesting challenge consists, for example, of standing on one leg on the tube or bus and trying to stay upright

for as long as possible. Once you've mastered this, the challenge can be increased by closing your eyes. Only do this if there is something to hold on to in case you should suddenly lose your balance.

The examples shown simply serve to illustrate the principle of a sensible exercise regime, which is tailored to the sport concerned and geared to reducing injuries. Training of this kind, if carried out on a regular basis and at suitable intervals between training on the water, is highly effective in preventing ankle joint and knee injuries. This is due to the fact that the body learns to react to external influences by means of quick compensatory movements. Take small wind waves for example, which make riding the wave more difficult. Following neuromuscular training undertaken continuously over a sufficient period, the athlete is better able to sense the effects of these small wind waves on his "overall system" – surfer-board-kite – and immediately execute small compensatory movements that enable him to maintain his balance. Thus it is not surprising that improving neuromuscular interaction results in kitesurfing that is not only safer, but also more coordinated and therefore more elegant.

Endurance training

Kitesurfing in the waves probably can't be classified as an endurance sport. But realizing that the level of exertion required causes muscle fatigue should be enough to motivate you to participate in regular endurance training. This fatigue occurs because the often sustained static loads that kitesurfing imposes on the body prevent the cardiovascular system's transport function from working to its full capacity. As a result, too little oxygen reaches the muscles involved, leading to anaerobic energy recovery. This produces lactate, which has to be removed in turn by the circulatory system. If both the supply of oxygen and the removal of by-

products such as lactate are limited, coordination is impaired and performance deteriorates also. If the cardiovascular system is functioning perfectly, however, the by-products of muscular exertion can be removed and oxygen supplied more quickly in the short phases when the muscles are relaxed. The muscles work more reliably and for longer, which is highly desirable if you don't want to be forced to bring the perfect day (which doesn't come around that often) to a premature end because you're out of shape.

To meet the demands that the above training activities place on you even over a longer period of time, you should go on endurance runs with the maximum proprioceptive content. Running on various surfaces such as sand, gravel, grass, etc. is suitable for this. Running barefoot also, sometimes with eyes closed, will better stimulate the perceptual capacity of the muscles, ligaments and joints as well as increasing endurance levels.

Excessively long runs are not recommended, since these would only cause your body unnecessary stress.[31] Instead, varied runs should be undertaken that address different energy recovery systems. Anaerobic and aerobic energy recovery are practised alternately by integrating dunes, hills or even stairs into the run. A suitable length training session should last no longer than 12-30 minutes. As your level of fitness improves after a few weeks, it's not the length of the runs that is increased, but the intensity.

---

[30] Cf. Nagel & Spreckels, 2003, p. 213.

[31] Verstegen, 2006, p. 184: "Each time he puts a foot on the ground the stress is as great as seven times your body weight."

9 Concluding comments

Using a kite in surfing is another milestone in the centuries-old history of the development of this once royal sport; whether it will be the last remains to be seen. Be that as it may, the possibilities that a new sport like this opens up are many and varied: crossing shorebreaks easily and reaching the ideal point of the wave for your ride are attractive features along with the extra energy that can be added to surfing by using a kite. It's this that makes the sport so incredibly interesting both for surfers and for kitesurfers coming from a freestyle background.

To ensure a trouble-free and above all safe introduction to kitesurfing in the waves, we've shown a wide range of options. Going about it in a structured manner starts with choosing a suitable location, selecting training content that is appropriate to your level of ability, the related visualization of this content in mental imaging and proceeding by way of the warm-up routine to the actual training session on the water. In addition, suitable complementary activities between kitesurfing sessions achieve rapid success in learning and reduce the risk of injury.

If you've taken all the advice given above to heart, you'll experience many wonderful days in the waves and be able to affirm the words spoken by Greg Noll, a big wave surfer of the first generation, 50 years ago: "The ride on the wave is such a reward that people gear their entire lives to it." And the wave-riding kings of Oceania would certainly have seen it that way too.

133

Bottom turn offshore.

Gear

Boards

The choice of board is crucial for manoeuvrability in the wave and depends on both the conditions and the rider's physique. Waveboards now come in many different shapes and sizes. The range extends from "production boards" from the major kite brands to countless "custom" boards from surfboard shapers, who are taking the waveboard in new directions with ever newer shapes and styles. In parallel to the development of kitesurfing in the waves, the development of the wave kite board has received a huge boost in the last couple of years. There are now very small, wide boards for small waves. For strapless riding, there are medium-sized boards of different thicknesses and widths with a wide variety of tails for medium-sized waves, plus long, narrow boards for large and powerful waves.

When asked which is the right board for which conditions, every shaper has his own theory and will answer differently from another shaper. There will be plenty of experimenting in this field in the future too, which can only be good for the development of kitesurfing in the waves. But in general, it can be said that boards come in lengths of 5'0"–6'6" and are typically measured in feet, a practice adopted from surfing. The boards closely resemble those of the parent sport and can only be ridden in one direction, with a nose and a tail. Fins are positioned to the rear of the waveboard, so that the kiter's back foot is located over these. A lot of experiments have been conducted with regard to the number and positioning of fins. Following various tests with a single fin right up to four fins, boards with three fins have tended to be the most popular up to now.

The choice of board is dependent, as already stated, on the body weight of the kiter and the conditions. It is also dependent on your individual style and preferences when wave riding. If it's possible to try out a board before buying it, you should always do so. The general rule is: small, especially wide boards should be ridden in small waves, as these not only fit better into the small waves but their width makes it easy to kite strapless. Conversely, long, narrow boards should be used in big waves, as these are fast and so remain stable in fast, "powerful" waves. Medium-sized boards measuring 5'6" for particularly light riders up to 6'3" for heavier riders, with widths of between 17" and 19", are the most common boards for medium wave sizes and have good all-round attributes.

Furthermore, boards differ in terms of their method of construction. Many different surfboard designs are now available. Board manufacturers are experimenting not just with wood but also with, for example, carbon, and a steady stream of new designs are being trialled. Many riders and shapers swear by a particular design, but here too it's ultimately a question of personal taste. And in spite of the many constructions available, for most kiters the good old

Different tails, along with the volume and width of the board, influence its ride attributes.

Riders of different heights and weights require boards of differing lengths and widths.

polyester-fibreglass surfboard is still the most comfortable, because with a few exceptions, these are more pleasant to ride than production boards.

Board set-up

For riders who wish to ride strapless and in small waves, the set-up is quite easy because they don't have to attach any footstraps. For everyone else, positioning the footstraps is a highly individual affair, which can take some time before the ideal position is found.

There are riders who prefer a wider stance (the distance between the feet), just as there are some who feel more comfortable with a smaller space between the feet on the board. Furthermore, there are wave kiters who would rather stand further forward, while there are others who prefer to stand further back on the board. The rule of thumb here is: the further back the rider or his back foot is positioned, the more sharply and "aggressively" the turns can be ridden, as more pressure can be exerted on the tail and the fins, enabling the tail to be "pushed round" more easily. The further forward you stand on the board, the more drawn-out and softer the manoeuvres become, as you ride more over the entire edge of the board than just over the tail. Most wave kiters place their rear footstrap so that their foot is between the rear fin and the two front fins. The front footstrap is then positioned forward of this at a distance that is comfortable for the front foot.

Fins

As if choosing a board isn't complicated enough, a huge variety of different fins are also available, and these can have a strong influence on the surfing attributes of the board. Four types of fin boxes are widely available. The fin box on the board dictates which type of fin is used:

1. **Glass-on fins:** These are the original type of fin and stem from the "olden"

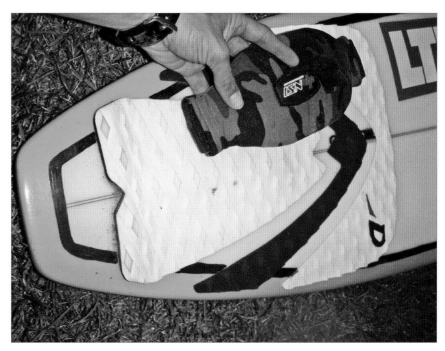

Diffferent inserts permit variable footstrap positioning.

days of surfing. Here the fin is laminated directly onto the board and cannot be removed. This type of fin is extremely impractical if you intend to travel. In spite of this, some boards with fixed laminated fins can still be found on the world's beaches.

2. **FCS:** These fin boxes and fins are widespread. Their big advantage is the ease with which they can be removed and replaced. This makes it easy to try out one of the many fin models available from FCS and also to be able to simply pack your board in your board bag minus fins, which saves them from becoming damaged and facilitates travelling.

3. **Future fins:** The Future fin system is also pretty widespread and offers the advantage that the fins can be removed from the board. The Future box is very stable and is best recommended for kiteboards, as wave kiters normally travel at very high speed and so the

pressure on the fins is very high. Future also markets a large range of different fins.

4. **Mini tuttle:** This fin box is widespread among the production boards of the major board manufacturers. These fins too are easy to remove and the fin

Future fins are easy to insert and remove and have a stable fin box.

boxes are very stable and durable, like the fins themselves. Unfortunately, mini-tuttle fins are very hard to find and are not obtainable in surf shops. Therefore, you should always pack an extra set of fins in your luggage. The range of mini-tuttle fins is not very large either.

> **Tip:** Riders who use FCS or Future fins have a choice of various sizes, different flex and various shapes of fins. Once again, personal taste is the deciding factor here. Normally, however, a "high-speed" fin or a "tow-surfing" fin is good for kitesurfing in the waves. The flex of the fin sometimes makes it easier to push the board into the turn.

Kites

The high depower characteristics of the kites now make it possible to kite in spots and conditions in which you couldn't kite previously due to the difficult wind conditions. A kite with lots of depower makes it easier to "turn on and off" the power of the kite while riding a wave. This gives a feel very similar to surfing. You can "power" the kite through a bottom turn, for example, and when turning up the wave at high speed take the pressure almost completely out of the kite in order to execute a vertical top turn that is very similar to that of surfers. Older kites with little depower (C-kites) make it pretty difficult for a kiter to ride a wave top to bottom, as he must battle against the constant pull of the kite, which aims to pull him automatically out of the "critical" wave sections. Naturally, this doesn't mean that it's impossible to ride a wave using a C-kite, just that these kites make the manoeuvre in the wave considerably more difficult.

Many manufacturers offer a large number of kites that have a significant depower effect. The torment of making a choice is worse because every kite has somewhat different riding attributes. For kitesurfing in particular, fast turning kites

are highly suitable, because these make it possible to steer the kite quickly to where you need it in anticipation of the next turn. Accordingly, riding waves with a small kite (5–9 m²) is generally easier. However, this large range includes faster and slower kites. Many kites have an adjustment setting for the "turning speed" and it is advisable to set this to "fast". The following two kite shapes are especially recommended for :[32]

Bow kite

Currently the most widespread form of kite, the bow kite not only makes kiting considerably safer, but also much more comfortable. Bow kites come in a wide variety of forms and are mostly equipped with a bridle-pulley system, which enables the angle of attack of the kite to be changed more than on normal C-kites. The result is that the kite can be almost completely "depowered", which is an enormous advantage especially in waves. The application range of a bow kite is extremely large, because it can be flown in the lower wind range and can be controlled well right into the high wind range. Most bow kites are fitted with four lines.

---

[32] Further information on kite shapes, the kite set-up and kite repair can be found in the first part of our book, *Kitesurfing: The Complete Guide*.

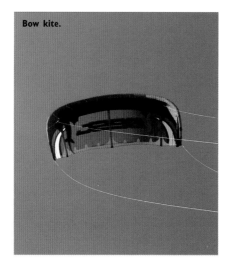

Bow kite.

Hybrid kite

If the switch from a C-kite to a bow kite is too extreme for your liking, then the hybrid kite offers a compromise. These kites have a flatter arch and have mostly round wing tips. Hybrid kites are not fitted with pulleys for the most part, but in some cases are equipped with bridles. Different manufacturers are working on widely ranging designs and ideas, and development is ongoing. Compared with a normal C-kite, the application range has been considerably extended, with a very positive effect on kitesurfing in the waves. Even the turning attributes of hybrid kites are very good in most cases. These kites have four or five lines.

Five-line kite.

Miscellaneous

Bar and quick release

It's best to get the bar that goes with the kite, as each manufacturer coordinates its system components. The quick release function is then also guaranteed, which is especially important in wave riding. No kiter should go into the waves without an operational safety system. Operating the system should be easy and it should be tested in advance, because out in the waves surprising situations can always arise in which you must be able to release yourself very quickly from the kite. With regard to the wide variety of bars and QR systems on the market, one thing should be borne in mind: the simpler the QR is to operate, the better.

Leash

In waves, it is generally advisable not to use a leash or line. In big waves especially, it can be the case in emergencies that you need to release yourself from the kite quickly. Sometimes it can take too long to operate both the quick release and a leash in this situation. The leash can also pose an additional hazard if the rider finds himself in the wave with a dropped kite, because he then has to keep an eye on the lines and stay clear of them, and an additional "line" would only complicate the situation further. A leash should only be used in very small waves and onshore conditions for trying out unhooked manoeuvres.

Harness

Wave kiters normally use waist harnesses for a comfortable ride in waves. It gives the rider more freedom of movement, which is essential in surfing. Another practical advantage of the waist harness over the seat harness is that you can swim more easily in it, which can be extremely useful in waves.

Wax

Surf wax is an ingenious invention by surfers and is also used in kitesurfing in the waves to render certain areas of the board non-slip. On small, strapless boards wax can sometimes replace a footpad. On larger boards, wax can be applied between the footpads, making foot changes easier and preventing slipping during the switchover. There are various brands of surf wax for use in different water temperatures, something worth bearing in mind when buying wax.

137

Book team

Kristin Boese has made a name for herself in the kiting world as a two-time world champion in the freestyle discipline. After discovering the enormous diversity offered by the sport of kiting and also a love of waves, she went in a new direction in competitions and not only became overall world champion in 2007, but has now also taken the world title in the wave discipline. With eight world titles in various disciplines gained in four consecutive years, Kristin has followed the current trends in the sport of kiting. Kitesurfing in the waves has given her an entirely new perspective and fresh motivation.

Her sponsors Best Kiteboarding, RIAL and Air Berlin support her on her travels and also helped make this book *Kitesurfing in the Waves: The Complete Guide* possible.

Sky Solbach is one of the world's best wave kiters. Raised on the Caribbean island of Bonaire, he learned to read waves in his early childhood and was instantly at home on a surfboard. As a professional kiter, he first proved his capabilities in the freestyle field and to date he is one of only two Americans ever to have won a World Cup. For the last three years Sky has been concentrating exclusively on kitesurfing in the waves and has made a major contribution to the current popularity of this discipline. He attracts considerable attention with his "powerful" style in big waves and the unbelievable effortlessness with which he performs strapless manoeuvres; he is frequently asked to explain precisely how a particular manoeuvre works. As the "guest star" in this book, he now passes on his knowledge to others. Last but not least, Sky is also responsible in part for Kristin's new-found love of waves and is thus indispensable to this book. His sponsors are North Kiteboarding, Delta Boards and ION.

Christian Spreckels has degrees in sport science and psychology. He is an assistant lecturer at the University of Hamburg and also coaches in various sports. His favourite sport is surfing, which he took up 23 years ago, and he has also been an enthusiastic kitesurfer for the last eight years.

Photographs:
Ian Trafford
Kim Kern
John Bilderback
Russel Ord
Gavin Buttler
Evan Mckay
Carlos Delicato
Lance Koudele
Jody MacDonald
Sharkeye/Reload Production
Carola Foermer
Stephen Whitesell
Karen Hauser
Just Be

Illustrations:
Maike Lund

Special thanks

Special thanks go to Ian Trafford, Jody MacDonald and Kim Kern for the many hours they spent behind the camera and also for the emotional support they provided. I'd also like to thank Marti Littlewood of Delta Designs for the amazing surfboard designs and Sky for the terrific help he has given me over the last few years in getting into kitesurfing in the waves, as well as for his endless patience while the text was being written and during the photoshoots. Sincere thanks also to Maike Lund, without whom it would not have been possible to put the sequences together; and to my sponsors Best Kiteboarding, RIAL and Air Berlin, without whose assistance this second volume would not have appeared. And last but not least, I want to thank Christian Spreckels as without his ideas, motivation and unbelievably diligent work this book would never even have been started.

Kristin Boese

I would like to give special thanks to Kristin once again for her fantastic and dependable cooperation and to Sky Solbach for his commitment and gracious participation in the creation of this book. A special thank you also to my small daughter Johanna for her cute smile and to Lili for her cheerful nature, both of which were a great motivation. I am also indebted to Frieder Bachteler and Hauke Bischoff for their critical comments and corrections, and to Maike Lund for her professional editing of the sequences and graphics.

Christian Spreckels

Bibliography

Alfermann, D. & Stoll, O., *Sportpsychologie. Ein Lehrbuch in 12 Lektionen*. Aachen 2005. (Sports psychology. A textbook in 12 lessons)

Bierhoff-Alfermann, D., *Sportpsychologie*. Stuttgart 1986. (Sports psychology)

Buchbauer, J., *Präventives Training zur Behebung von Haltungsfehlern*, 2nd edition. Schorndorf 2001. (Preventive training to rectify posture faults)

Csikszentmihalyi, M., *Das flow-Erlebnis. Jenseits von Angst und Langeweile: im Tun aufgehen*, 7th edition. Stuttgart 1999. (Beyond boredom and anxiety: Experiencing flow in work and play)

Daugs, R., Einige Bemerkungen zum Beitrag von Horst Tiwald "Zur Theorie des Mentalen Trainings". In: *Leibeserziehung-Leibesübung*, Vol. 26(9), 1972, 194–195. (Some comments on the article by Horst Tiwald "On the theory of mental imaging")

Eberspächer, H., *Mentale Trainingsformen in der Praxis*. Oberhaching 1990. (Mental imaging forms in practice)

Fetz, F., Mentale Trainingsmethoden. In: *Praxis der Leibesübungen*, 14 (1973), pp. 51–56. (Mental imaging methods)

Fodor, J.A., *The modularity of mind*. Cambridge 1983.

Gabler, W., Hauser, H., Hug, O. & Steiner, H. (Hg.), *Psychologische Beratung und Diagnostik und Beratung im Leistungssport*. Frankfurt 1985. (Psychological consultancy and diagnostics in performance sport)

Geiger, U. & Schmid, C., *Muskeltraining mit dem Thera-Band*. Munich 2004. (Muscle training using the Thera-Band)

Groos, K., *The Play of Man*. New York 1901.

Hebbel-Seeger, A., *Snowboarding. Guide to Ride*. Aachen 2001.

Hossner, E.-J., Beim Fertigkeitslernen im Sport: Keine Angst vor Überforderungen! *Sportpsychologie*, Vol. 7(2), 1993, 17–20. (Learning skills in sport: No fear of being overchallenged!)

Kröger, G., *Wellenreiten. Ein ethnologischer Beitrag zur Geschichte des Wellenreitens. Hausarbeit zur Erlangung des Magistergrades*. Institut für Völkerkunde, Göttingen 1979. (Surfing. An ethnological contribution on the history of surfing. Thesis to gain a Masters degree)

Leist, K.-H., Transfer beim Erwerb von Bewegungskönnen. In: *Sportwissenschaft* Vol. 4(2), 1974, 136–163. (Transfer in the acquisition of movement prowess)

Leist, K.-H., *Lernfeld Sport*. Cologne 1993. (Sport as a development field)

Lenk, H., *Leistungssport: Ideologie oder Mythos?* Stuttgart 1972.

Michaelis, P., *Moderne funktionelle Gymnastik*. Aachen 2000. (Modern functional gymnastics)

Nagel, V. & Spreckels, C., *Mit Ballspielen zum Tennis*. Aachen 2003. (Through ball games to tennis)

Nickel, C., Zernial, O., Musahl, V., Hansen, U., Zantop, P. & Petersen, W., Prospective study of kitesurfing injuries. *Am J Sports Med*, Vol. 32(4), 2004, 921–927.

Petersen, W., Hansen, U., Zernial, O. et al., Mechanism and prevention of kitesurfing injuries (in German). *Sportverletzung-Sportschaden*, Vol. 16, 2002, 115–121.

Petersen, W., Zantop, T., Steensen, M., Hypa, A., Wessolowski, T. & Hassenpflug, J., Prävention von Verletzungen der unteren Extremität im Handball: Erste Ergebnisse des Kieler Handball-Verletzungs-Präventionsprograms. *Sportverletzung-Sportschaden*, Vol. 16(3), 2002, 122–126. (Prevention of lower limb injuries in handball: Initial results of the Kiel Handball Injury Prevention Program)

Spreckels, C., *Kitesurfing with Kristin Boese. The world champion's training program.* Stuttgart 2007.

Stow, D., *Encyclopaedia of the oceans.* London 2004.

Syer, J. & Connolly, C., *Sporting Body, Sporting Mind.* Cambridge 1984.

Syer, J. & Connolly, C., *Psychotraining für Sportler.* Reinbek 1987. (Psychotraining for athletes)

Tiwald, H., Zur Theorie des Mentalen Trainings. In: *Leibeserziehung-Leibesübung*, 26. Jg., 1972, Heft 5, 98–102. (On the theory of mental imaging)

Tiwald, H., "Mentales Training". Erwiderung auf die Kritik von Daugs. In: *Leibeserziehung-Leibesübung*, 26. Jg., 1972, Heft 9, 196. ("Mental imaging". Reply to the criticism by Daugs)

Tiwald, H., Mentales Training und sportliche Leistungsfähigkeit. In: *Leibeserziehung-Leibesübung*, Vol. 27(3), 1973, 56–60. (Mental imaging and athletic performance)

Verstegen, M. & Williams, P., *Core performance.* Munich 2006.

Volpert, W., *Optimierung von Trainingsprogramn; Untersuchungen über den Einsatz des mentalen Trainings beim Erwerb sensomotorischer Fertigkeit*, 2nd edition. Lollar/Lahn 1976. (Optimising training programs; Studies on the use of mental imaging in the acquisition of sensomotory skill)

Wiemann, K., Untersuchungen zum mentalen Training turnerischer Bewegungsabläufe. In: *Die Leibeserziehung*, Vol. 20(2), 1971, 36–41. (Studies on the mental imaging of gymnastic movement sequences)

Ziegler, M., Kwiatowsky, A., Reer, R. & Braumann, K. M., Verletzungen beim Kitesurfen, Ursachen & Präventionsmöglichkeiten. *Deutsche Zeitschrift für Sportmedizin*, 56(7/8), 2005, 256. (Injuries in kitesurfing, causes and options for prevention)

141

Picture credits:

John Bilderback: page 17, 63, 78/79, 80/81, 102/103, 122/123

Kristin Boese: page 134, 135, 136

Toby Bromwich: page 124

Gavin Butler: page 2, 50

Carlos Delicato: 25, 28/29, 108, 127(bottom), 139

Carola Foermer: page 20, 129, 130

Karen Hauser: page 138 (left)

Just Be: page138 (right)

Kim Kern: page 5 (top), 30, 31, 41 (big picture), 54/55, 66/67, 68, 70/71, 87, 88/89, 92/93,

Jody MacDonald: front cover, page 9, 23, 36, 48/49, 52, 62, 72/73, 74/75, 76/77, 94/95, 98/99, 100/101

Evan Mckay: page 44/45

NASA: page 11

North Kiteboarding: page 138 (middle)

Russel Ord: page 6, 29, 65

Sharkeye/Reload Productions: page 5 (middle), 27, 60/61, 82/83, 84/85, 86, 104/105, 106/107

Sky Solbach: page 5 (bottom), 41 (small picture), 126, 127 (small picture)

Ian Trafford: page 22, 32/33, 34/35, 37, 38, 39, 40/41, 46/47, 53, 56/57, 69, 90/91, 109, 110/111, 112/113, 114/115, 116/117, 120/121

Stephen Whitesell: 133

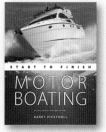